Pathology & Aesthetics

Essays on the Pathological in Kant and Contemporary Aesthetics

d|u|p

materialisierungen 4

Andrea von Hülsen-Esch, Ricarda Bauschke-Hartung, Vittoria Borsò, Reinhold Görling, Hans Körner, Achim Landwehr, Roger Lüdeke, Eva Schlotheuber, Timo Skrandies, Jürgen Wiener (Hg.)

graduiertenkolleg
materialität und produktion

DFG

Edited by Louis Schreel

Pathology & Aesthetics

Essays on the Pathological in Kant and Contemporary Aesthetics

HEINRICH HEINE
UNIVERSITÄT DÜSSELDORF

d|u|p

Bibliografische Information der Deutschen Nationalbibliothek
Die Deutsche Nationalbibliothek verzeichnet diese Publikation in der Deutschen Nationalbibliografie; detaillierte bibliografische Daten sind im Internet über http://dnb.dnb.de abrufbar.

http://www.dupress.de
Redaktion: Louis Schreel
Lektorat: Marnie Slater & Liz Allen
Titelbild: Etna © Petra Poggenpohl
Satz, Layout und Umschlaggestaltung: Hannah Reller
Herstellung: docupoint GmbH, Barleben

Der Fließtext ist gesetzt in Adobe Garamond Pro
ISBN: 978-3-95758-032-0

Table of Contents

Preface: Pathology and Aesthetics

Louis Schreel

Unlike current usages of the term, Kant uses "pathological" not as the opposite of the normal, something dangerously irrational or (psychologically) diseased. On the contrary, for Kant, it is our everyday, normal actions that are more or less always pathological. Behavior is pathological whenever something (a *"Triebfeder"*)—ranging from the most basic need to the most elevated and abstract idea—is driving our actions. In other words, when the mind follows the attraction of an inclination, of an empirical interest, it is "pathological." Kant opposes to the pathological the purely formal, autonomous determination of the will, in which he situates human freedom. The driving force corresponding to the latter is not an inclination, but "a respect for something entirely different from life, something much more worthy than life and its enjoyment": duty as the supra-sensual nature of the genuine drive (*"echte Triebfeder"*) of practical reason.

As is well known, this discovery of the ethical condition through the withdrawal from the realm of material objects, the discovery of the "pure" *sollen*, "before" every object, through the uniquely human faculty of abstraction, has had a strong impact on the way in which the *Critique of the Power of Judgment* would conceptualize the respective ("higher") feelings of beauty and the sublime. Just as many of his eighteenth-century predecessors and contemporaries, Kant discarded the matter of sensation as a potential danger to aesthetic contemplation, feeding rather what might be called a pathological art. Many of his nineteenth- and twentieth-century successors, however, argued that such a purely formalist account of aesthetic experience based on speculative and pragmatic functions of the subject failed to account for the particular intensity and worldly embeddedness of aesthetic affections.

German idealists, such as Fichte, Schelling and Hölderlin, and contemporary (art) philosophers, such as, for example, Jacques Lacan and Gilles Deleuze, start exactly with a reassessment and profound reinterpretation of the German term *Empfindung*. It is remarkable how this is often connected to a meditation on suffering and pathology. Rather than being a higher *Geistesgefühl* (Kant), the aesthetic dimension would be of an essentially affective nature: it concerns an event that affects us and that discloses no intentional structure whatsoever. One can discern in this evolution a return to the original Greek meaning of the terms *pathè, pathèma* and *pathos*, namely *the undergoing of an event that happens to us*. The oldest meaning of these words is *suffering, sickness* and *bodily ache*. It is remarkable that many contemporary authors prefer negative affects (such as disgust, fear and a correlated *Angstbereitschaft*) over more euphoric affects when the disclosure-character of art is concerned. Astonishment seems more like a wound than like a wonder. For example, in Deleuze's view of the artist as a symptomatologist, "a clinician of civilization," art must extract us from our habitual, dogmatic correlations with the world and reveal how the body as pure vitality and thus as pure pathos puts the organic-organized body under pressure. The shock with which art forces thought to abandon its merely abstract possibilities and effectively realize itself through a connection to reality, is for Deleuze necessarily a *violent* one, and is conceptualized using (and transforming) a range of psychiatric pathologies (e. g. hysteria and schizophrenia). In light of these recent developments, we focus in this collection of essays on aesthetic implementations of pathology and their way of determining pathology not (only) in a negative way, as deficiency, but also in a positive, constructive manner, furnishing philosophy the paradigm of a renewed subjectivity, of a new way of being oneself.

The volume collects papers presented at a symposium entitled *Pathology and Aesthetics. The Concept of the Pathological in Kant and Contemporary Aesthetics*, held in Düsseldorf in December 2014 by the graduate school Materiality and Production, of the Heinrich-Heine Universität Düsseldorf. Both the symposium and the present collection of essays were made possible with the financial support of the DFG (Deutsche Forschungsgemeinschaft / German Research Foundation).

Kant's Apathology of Compassion

1

Wolfram Bergande

> Now reason's ability to become master over all the inclinations striving against it through the mere idea of a law is absolutely inexplicable, hence it is also incomprehensible how the senses could have the ability to become master over a reason which commands with such authority on its side. For if all the world proceeded in accordance with the precept of the law, we would say that everything occurred according to the order of nature, and nobody would think even of inquiring after the cause.
> —Immanuel Kant, *Religion within the boundaries of mere reason*[1]

> Christianity has assuredly taught men to pay little attention to God's jouissance, and this is how Kant makes pass his voluntarism of Law-for-Law's-sake, which is something that tops, one might say, the ataraxia of the Stoic experience.
> —Lacan, *Kant with Sade*[2]

1. The Moral Pleasure of Respect

In his critical works, e. g. in the *Critique of Practical Reason,* Kant employs the well-known and seemingly clear-cut distinction between sensuousness, *Sinnlichkeit*, on the one hand and understanding, *Verstand*, respectively reason, *Vernunft*, on the other, hence between the "physical" (Kant 1889, pp. 122, 133) laws governing human nature and the moral law, the categorical imperative, which ought to govern the individual's will and thence, at least in principle, his or her acts, too.[3] Kant's moral philosophy accordingly seems to divide into two aspects: into what on the one hand could be called a pathology, taking care of reason as it tends to get heteronomously, i. e. sensuously affected or even passionately so; and, on the other, into what could not unjustly be called an 'apathology' which secures the grounds for an unaffected and dispassionate morality. This apathology comes close to a praxeology; even if Kant, unlike the Stoics or the Aristotelian-Thomistic tradition, does not

1 Kant 1996, p. 102f. (Footnote †); cf. Kant 2007, 06: 059.

2 Lacan 2006a, p. 651f. (Translation modified.)

3 Cf. Wood 2015, 132ff.

depart from an absolute Other (an almighty God) but only postulates his existence and his eventual afterworldly reward for a moral life.

For Kant, feelings, *Gefühle*, respectively sentiments, *Empfindungen*, almost invariably fall under physical laws, hence under the aspect of pathology. "[E]very feeling generally" (Kant 1889, p. 167) is "pathological" (ibid.), writes Kant in the second *Critique*, literally so because feelings ultimately derive from the subject's *pathè*, from its physical nature, and critically because they tend to encroach upon the autonomy of moral reason. However, already in the second *Critique* there is one—although only one single—exception to this rule: the "singular" "moral feeling" of "respect", *Achtung* (Kant 1889, p. 169). Being "produced simply by reason" (Kant 1889, p. 169), it is a case *sui generis*, even if compared with the somewhat similar aesthetic feelings which Kant will introduce only later in the *Critique of Judgement*.[4] Standing out as an exceptionally "practical" (Kant 1889, p. 172f.) feeling, respect accompanies those and only those wills which are morally good because they would be grounded in pure reason. Practically, this means that the will in question would be absolutely cleansed even of the "slightest admixture" (Kant 1889, p. 112) of pathological (sentimental, as it were) causality. As a matter of fact, later, in the Critique of Judgement, Kant will explicate that actually "any determination of the will" as such would carry a "state of mind which accompanies" it; and that this state of mind "is in itself a feeling of pleasure and identical with it" (Kant 1914, p. 70).[5] So is respect, *Achtung*, then a pleasure? Kant's answer must appear somewhat paradoxical: yes and no. Yes, because given that respect is a determination of the will, it must be identical with a feeling of

[4] Cf. Kant 1886, p. 115: It "is entirely of its own kind".

[5] Cf. Kant 1914, p. 53: "But to will something, and to have a satisfaction in its existence, i. e. to take an interest in it, are identical."

pleasure, too. No, because the feeling of respect actually suggests itself as exemplary for the "moral pleasure [*moralischen Lust*]" (Kant 2007, 06: 378, 391; Kant 1889, pp. 289, 301) of which Kant writes in 1797 in the *Metaphysic of Ethics*; and as 'moral pleasure' respect is far from being a pleasure in the ordinary sense of the term.

This is because the determination of the will by the "practical law" (Kant 1889, p. 112), which occasions the feeling of respect, makes a very special case for Kant. Even if one insisted on calling respect a 'pleasure', namely a 'moral pleasure', it nevertheless would not involve any kind of 'pathological' pleasure, neither in the sense of presupposing it, nor of feeding on it, nor of aiming at it. As Kant claims in the *Critique of Practical Reason*:

> Reason, with its practical law, determines the will immediately, not by means of an intervening feeling of pleasure or pain, not even of pleasure in the law itself [*nicht vermittelst eines dazwischen kommenden Gefühls der Lust und Unlust, selbst nicht an diesem Gesetze*], and it is only because it can, as pure reason, be practical, that it is possible for it to be legislative (ibid.; Kant 2007, 05: 025).

Nor is respect itself, as seems to go without saying at this point in Kant's text, a pathological 'pleasure in the law itself' either. All of this holds true for Kant even though the determination of the will, as he admits, implies a somewhat painful feeling of "humiliation" of one's "self-conceit" (Kant 1889, p. 167)[6], a feeling of pain which, although it is not a pleasure, would have to count as "pathological" (ibid.) in equal measure, if only it was not indeed the negative reverse of the feeling of respect and thus, according to Kant, another major "effect of the consciousness of the moral law" (ibid.).[7]

So not only is it that the moral feeling of respect would not in any way involve or imply 'pathological' feelings. What is more, it "cannot be compared to any patho-

[6] Cf. Kant 1889, p. 173.

[7] Cf. Kant 1889, p. 213.

logical feeling" (ibid., p. 169) in the first place, let alone itself be "reckoned either as pleasure or pain" (ibid., p. 173) in the ordinary, 'pathological' sense, for it "[...] is a feeling that applies merely to what is practical, and depends on the conception of a law, simply as to its form, not on account of any object [...]" (ibid.). It is "produced by an intellectual cause" only (Kant 1889, p. 166). And that is also why it "is the only one that we know quite a priori, and the necessity of which we can discern [*einsehen können*]" (ibid.).[8] So much does respect grow from purely reasonable grounds alone that even though for the sake of convenience one might call it a 'moral pleasure' it nevertheless and strictly speaking "contains no pleasure" (Kant 1889, p. 173) at all (nor pain, at least if we leave its negative reverse, humiliation, aside).

What the feeling of respect actually does consist of phenomenologically speaking is, according to Kant, a certain kind of "*self-approbation*" which "contains something *elevating*" (ibid.), a kind of "inward peace" (Kant 1889, p. 181).[9] More precisely, it is a "contentment, which is primarily contentment with one's own person" (ibid., p. 215), however far from it's opposite double: complacency, *Behaglichkeit*. This contentment or self-contentment may certainly amount to some kind of "enjoyment" (ibid.), as Kant admits. However, "contentment (*acquiescentia*)" in the full meaning of the term is "unattainable" for human beings "during life" (Kant 2006, p. 130). And, what is more, the contentment that is eventually attainable for humans is only "a negative satisfaction with one's state" (Kant 1889, p. 215). It yields an only negative enjoyment, one which has "nothing to do with enjoyment of life" (ibid., p. 183) in the ordinary sense and

8 Translation modified.

9 Kant also writes of a "*Vernunftliebe seiner selbst*", footnote ** in Kant 2007, 06: 045.

> [...] which cannot be called happiness, because it does not depend on the positive concurrence of a feeling, nor is it, strictly speaking, bliss, since it does not include complete independence on inclinations and wants, but it resembles bliss in so far as the determination of one's will at least can hold itself free from their influence; and thus, at least in its origin, this enjoyment is analogous to the self-sufficiency which we can ascribe only to the Supreme Being (ibid., p. 215).

For the worldly human being who seeks to practically emulate this self-sufficient Supreme Being, contentment spells out as the moral virtue of "apathy" (Kant 2006, p. 152) or "equanimity" (Kant 2006, p. 131), rarely also as: "ataraxia, *Ataraxia*" (Kant 2006, p. 154; Kant 2007, 07: 256).[10] Kant repeatedly recommends or even commands apathy (e. g.: the "duty of apathy" (Kant 1886, p. 226) in the *Metaphysics of Ethics* (1797)), usually with an explicit reference to ancient Stoicism, like in the following passage from the *Anthropology from a Pragmatic Point of View* (1798):

> The principle of apathy—namely that the wise man must never be in a state of affect, not even in that of compassion with the misfortune of his best friend, is an entirely correct and sublime moral principle of the Stoic school; for affect makes us (more or less) blind (Kant 2006, p. 152).

If the twin feelings of humiliation-and-respect together make up the moral contentment of the human being, then we could say that something like countenance (like 'contentment' deriving from the Latin *continere*, 'to hold together, to enclose') is the respective practical disposition of an individual's "moral *ascetics*" (Kant 2005, p. 597; Kant 2007, 6: 484). In the *Metaphysics of Ethics*, Kant refers this "cultivation of virtue" (ibid.) to "the old watchword of the Stoa [...], *bear* and *forbear*: bear, endure the evils of life without complaint; forbear, abstain from its superfluous enjoyments [*überflüssigen Ergötzlichkeiten*]" (Kant 1886, p. 304). The virtuous human being ought to stay apathetic in the face of pathology, i. e. in the face of any sentiments/feelings, affects and passions, whether pleasurable or painful. This is because they constantly threaten to infringe upon the purely moral determination of the will.

---

[10] Cf. "Ataraxia" in Kant 2007, 07: 256. On "ataraxia" as *"Gleichmüthigkeit"* (equanimity) see: "Entwürfe zu dem Colleg über Anthropologie aus den 70er und 80er Jahren" (Kant 2007, p. 15: 854).

Sure enough, this does not mean to be "dull" or "indifferent" (Kant 2006, p. 131), as Kant hastens to add in the *Anthropology*.

However, it can lead to quite extreme consequences. Kant's notorious example, which appears in both the *Anthropology* (Kant 2007, 07: 253; Kant 2006, p. 152) and the *Metaphysics of Ethics* (Kant 2007, 06: 457; Kant 1886, p. 276), is the rejection of compassion, *Mitleid*, as a form of pathological suffering. Kant's referee in the *Metaphysics* is again the Stoic "sage" who "rejected compassion [*Mitleidenschaft*]" even in "the case of his friend" because he could not "allow" himself—and as to Kant indeed he ought not to allow himself—"to be infected by his [friend's] sorrow" and thus to "augment the evils in the world" (ibid.) by suffering together with him.[11] For the Kant of the *Metaphysics* this is tantamount to saying that as a matter of principle "there can be no obligation to act kindly out of compassion [*Mitleid*]" (ibid.).[12]

2. Compassion as Surrogate of Reason

But this is not the whole story. For in the *Anthropology*, Kant continues the above quoted passage about the 'principle of apathy' with an important reservation:

> Nevertheless the wisdom of nature has planted in us the predisposition to compassion in order to handle the reins provisionally, until reason has achieved the necessary strength; that is to say, for the purpose of enlivening us, nature has added the incentive of pathological (sensible) [*pathologischen (sinnlichen)*] impulse to the moral incentives for the good, as a temporary surrogate of reason [*einstweiliges Surrogat der Vernunft*] (Kant 2006, p. 152).

And in the *Metaphysics of Ethics*, in a section titled *Of the Duty of Sympathy*, Kant continues the discussion of this "predisposition of nature", namely of the natural predisposition "to have a fellow-feeling with the joys and sorrows [*Mitfreude und Mitleid (sympathia moralis)*] of others [*Anderer*]" (Kant 1886, p. 275; Kant 2007,

[11] Translation modified.

[12] Translation modified. Cf. Denis 2000.

06: 456).[13] Here, these two feelings, *Mitfreude* (compassionate joy, so to speak) and *Mitleid* (compassion), appear under the category of *"sympathia moralis"* (Kant 2007, 06: 456), which is somewhat paradoxical given that Kant maintains that we are undoubtedly dealing with sensuous feelings, *"sinnliche Gefühle"*, thus obviously not with moral but instead with aesthetical, *"ästhetisch"* (ibid.), i. e. with ultimately pathological feelings. This paradox notwithstanding, Kant infers from the 'predisposition of nature' to have such sympathetic feelings if not a direct 'obligation to act kindly out of compassion' (which, as we just have learned, cannot be) then nevertheless an "indirect duty [...] to cultivate the [se] sympathetic affections" (Kant 1886, p. 276).

So surprisingly here we are called on by Kant not to repress the naturally pathological feeling of *Mitleid*, compassion. Instead we are to cultivate it. To allow for this cultivation, Kant is led to introduce a further distinction between a natural and a cultivated kind of sympathy; this distinction temporarily resolves the paradoxical categorization just mentioned, it is true, but only at the cost of reapplying the primary distinction between morality and pathology, i. e. between *Achtung* (respect) and *Mitleid* (compassion or sympathy, respectively), within the subsphere of pathology itself, i. e. within the subsphere of compassion (respectively sympathy). So within this subsphere we face again the second *Critique's* primary distinction between morality and pathology: namely between a "free" and morally cultivated compassion which is 'participating' (*"theilnehmend"* (Kant 2007, 06: 456) and "seated in the will and the ability to communicate to one another" and which "depends on practical reason" (Kant 1886, p. 276)[14], if however, as we will learn, not on practical reason alone— and a slavish, *"servilis"* (Kant 2007, 06: 457), and pathologically admixed or soaked

[13] Translation modified.

[14] Translation modified.

compassion, a *"Mitleidenschaft"* (ibid.), which by contrast is "seated in that physical susceptibility, which nature has implanted in us, for feeling in common the delights or misery of our neighbour" (Kant 1886, p. 275f.). This latter *Mitleidenschaft* communicates itself by itself. By itself it is *"mittheilend"* (Kant 2007, 06: 457). It 'spreads in a natural way', *"sie sich ... natürlicher Weise verbreitet"*, comparable to 'warmth', *"Wärme"*, or 'contagious diseases', *"ansteckender Krankheiten"* (ibid.). By contrast to its counterpart, it is not a duty, not even an indirect one, but must remain repressed and avoided by all means.

So if there is, as we have learned in the *Anthropology*, 'the incentive of pathological (sensible) impulse to the moral incentives for the good, as a temporary surrogate of reason', then we can conclude from the *Metaphysics of Ethics* that this surrogate impulse is not straightforwardly pathological but the result of cultivation. And the *Metaphysics* seems to agree with the *Anthropology* as to why at all we should cultivate 'compassionate natural (aesthetical) affections', *"mitleidige natürliche (ästhetische) Gefühle"* (Kant 2007, 06: 457). We should do so because we can "[...] make them serve as instruments enabling us to discharge the offices of a humane mind, upon ethical principles [*sie als so viele Mittel zur Theilnehmung aus moralischen Grundsätzen und dem ihnen gemäßen Gefühl zu benutzen*]" (Kant 1886, p. 276). Particularly, we may use them in cases where practical reason is in need of support; for instance, as we read in the *Anthropology*, 'provisionally, until reason has achieved the necessary strength'. However, only insofar as they effectively serve such purposes should we cultivate them, that is, only insofar as they are directed to an active end. Otherwise they are useless, as Kant warns in the *Anthropology*: "[...] the ineffectual sharing of one's feelings [*die thatleere Theilnehmung seines Gefühls*] in order to appear sympathetically in tune with the feelings of others, thus allowing oneself to be affected in a merely passive way, is silly and childish" (Kant 2006, p. 132).

Still this is not the end of what can be termed Kant's apathology of compassion. If the *Metaphysics* calls on us to cultivate natural compassion, i. e. the sensuous sympathy with others: *"humanitas aesthetica"* (Kant 2007, 06: 456), and to transform it into truly humane compassion: *"humanitas practica"* (ibid.) as it 'depends on practical reason', then this is not so much because, as Kant considers, "we might be unable to repress" (Kant 1886, p. 277) it anyway; nor is it only because compassion can function as a temporary surrogate impulse for the possibly deficitary 'strength' of practical reason; rather, and this is astonishing, compassion can help us "to do what the representation of duty on its own might be unable to accomplish [*dasjenige zu tun, was die Pflichtvorstellung für sich allein nicht ausrichten würde*]" (ibid.)[15], as Kant surprisingly concedes towards the end of the *Metaphysics'* section on the *Duty of Sympathy*:

> Neither ought we to desert the chambers of the sick nor the cells of the debtor, in order to escape the painful sympathy we might be unable to repress, this emotion being a spring implanted in us by nature, prompting us to do what the representation of duty on its own might be unable to accomplish (Kant 1886, p. 276f.).[16]

There are—as Kant lets his readers know in what is a rather passing albeit concluding remark—actions commanded as duties by practical reason, and, as can be presumed, strengthfully so. Nevertheless, 'the representation of duty alone' does not suffice to determine the will effectively—presumably regardless of the support of the concomitant feeling of *Achtung*, respect. So obviously it is not only, as the *Anthropology* suggests, some temporary and hence sooner or later remediable deficit of

15 Translation modified.

16 Translation modified.

'the strength of reason' which compassion, the 'pathological surrogate of reason', is supposed to supplement in a however cultivated form. Rather, the *Metaphysics* seems to point here to a fundamental problem one might have with doing one's duty as it is commanded by the practical law alone. Can we not suspect that in extreme cases this problem might indeed become irremediable without the 'positive concurrence' of a cultivated 'pathological feeling'? And would not this consequently put the self-contentment of the virtuous agent in danger, together with the ideal of supreme self-sufficiency that orientates it?

One must be very precise here. Kant writes that "[...] although it is no direct duty to take a part in the joy or grief of others", it nevertheless "is a duty not to avoid" the occasions and places where such feelings are usually triggered: "the chambers of the sick" or the "cells of the debtor" (Kant 1886, p. 276). Even so, the feeling of the 'joy or grief of others' must remain problematic for Kant, like any of the other "inner and outer enjoyments" of everyday life: "only inasmuch as they are innocent in themselves, i. e., not contrary to morality, and present themselves spontaneously, may we adopt them, but never go in pursuit of them" (Kant 2001b, p. 397), as we learn from the notes taken by Johann Friedrich Vigilantius from Kant's lectures on ethics in 1793–94. Otherwise, Kant warns, they indeed might be "injurious to our self-contentment" (ibid.). As a consequence, it seems as if cases where cultivated compassion is asked for must neither actively be sought nor actively be avoided. If compassion arises, it must arise spontaneously, unintentionally. This probably also implies that such cases must not be passively sought nor be passively avoided either, i. e.: negligently or secretly. A perfectly balanced state of neither activity nor passivity is obviously what is at stake when it comes to the morally obligatory self-contentment of Kant's virtuoso of virtue.

Be this as it may, the remarkable result is that Kant seems to allow for cases where the 'representation of duty on its own' [*die Pflichtvorstellung für sich allein*], obviously because it is on its own, is not enough to determine the will; not just factually, e. g. because it would be overpowered by other pathological motives, *"Triebfedern"* (Kant 2007, 06: 036), or because it would lack the experience which enlivens or enhances its strength (and even granted that the effective outcome is always indeterminable because empirical), but principally—namely, as one may suspect, because without intuition the *Pflichtvorstellung* would be just as void, *"leer"* (Kant 2007, 03: 075) as it would then become "blind" or rather blinded under the rule of an uncultivated "affect" (Kant 2006, p. 152). Is this an overinterpretation? Certainly, Kant would have rejected any such interpretation, just like his *Metaphysics* explicitly opposes any such view. For if, according to Kant, "the power of mastering every opposing excitement of the sensory can, and indeed must, be absolutely postulated [*das Vermögen* (facultas) *der Überwindung aller sinnlich entgegenwirkenden Antriebe seiner Freiheit halber schlechthin vorausgesetzt werden kann und muß*]" (Kant 1886, p. 214f.; Kant 2007, 06: 397), then in principle reason must be the absolute master. Yet the question remains whether Kant's systematic treatment of compassion does not point to a fundamental problem with reason's principally absolute mastery, particularly in regard to Kant's famous coordination of freedom and constraint ('you can because you must'). The first epigraph to this text, taken from Kant's *Religion within the Boundaries of Mere Reason*, is one of a small number of scattered marginalia in Kant's corpus which appear to reflect such a problematic.

And yet recent secondary literature on Kant often appears to ignore this problematic. To give an example: It certainly is not altogether wrong to interpret Kant's text—as has been done—in the conventional sense that "only the moral feeling of *Achtung*, which is exclusively triggered by the practical law and which has an inner causal relation to the practical law, can guarantee that it only motivates to moral actions" (Goy 2007, p. 352). It is not wrong, but it understates the case, because, as has just been evidenced in Kant's text, there seem to be at least imaginable cases in which a 'temporary surrogate impulse' not only "may later facilitate our doing our duty" (Cartwright 1984, p. 87 Fn. 11) or cases in which it "can be of instrumental importance" (Denis 2000, p. 65), as other interpreters of Kant have it; but also cases in which such a surrogate impulse might be indispensable for doing our duties in the first place. A 'temporary surrogate impulse' then may be principally indispensable for a 'representation of duty' which, 'on its own' as it in some cases obviously is, without such an impulse, without an as it were Fichtean *"Anstoß"* (Fichte 2013, p. 37) *avant la lettre*, cannot perform its moral duty.[17] (And then again, if there indeed are such exceptional cases in which moral reason principally cannot dispense of this surrogate impulse, then of course the question arises as to how *Achtung* should be able to 'guarantee that it only motivates to moral actions' in all the other cases.)

Now on the other hand it is not only to overstate the case but just wrong to argue (as has been done by one interpreter in the recently published *Kant-Lexikon*) that "the natural feelings of compassion [*die natürlichen Gefühle des Mitleids*]" would be "necessary conditions of the accomplishment of charity [*notwendigen Bedingungen zur Erfüllung der Wohltätigkeit*]", even granted that they are "not sufficient for the

[17] Cf. Honneth 2001.

accomplishment of the moral duty of charity [*nicht hinreichend zur Erfüllung der moralischen Pflicht zur Wohltätigkeit*]" (Mieth 2015, p. 413).[18] Natural compassion is a condition of cultivated compassion, so much is true. Just like "[...] the sensible feeling which is at the bottom of all our inclinations is the condition of that impression which we call respect, *Achtung*" (Kant 1889, p. 168; Kant 2007, 05: 075) according to the *Critique of Practical Reason*. But in the *Metaphysics* Kant is quite clear about that "painful sympathy [*schmerzhaften Mitgefühl*] [...] being a spring [*einer der... Antriebe*] implanted in us by nature" (Kant 1886, p. 277): It is one of the springs to do good, *einer der Antriebe*, not the only one. Hence compassion (*Mitleid* respectively *Mitgefühl*), whether in natural or cultivated form, cannot be a necessary, i. e. a general condition of charity; nor can any other feeling be such a necessary condition, except *Achtung*. In the second *Critique*, Kant leaves no doubt about it: "There is here in the subject no antecedent feeling tending to morality. For this is impossible, since every feeling is sensuous, and the motive of moral intention must be free from all sensuous conditions [*die Triebfeder der sittlichen Gesinnung aber muß von aller sinnlichen Bedingung frei sein*]" (Kant 1889, p. 168).[19] Otherwise there could actually be no cases at all in which, as Kant claims, moral "[r]eason, with its practical law, determines the will immediately, not by means of an intervening feeling of pleasure or pain, not even of pleasure in the law itself, [...]" (ibid., p. 112). And according to Kant "practical pure reason" does determine the will, not only immediately but also effectively. It is not only the "objective determining principle of the objects of action as called good and evil" but also the "subjective determining principle, that is, a motive [*Triebfeder*] to this action [...]" (ibid., p. 168; Kant 2007, 05: 075).

[18] My translation.

[19] Translation modified.

As a result, compassion, i. e. the pathological affection, if not infectedness, by somebody else's feelings, appears as quite paradoxical, as quite Rousseauistic so to speak, at least in these two ultimate publications of Kant, the *Metaphysics* and the *Anthropology*. Both inessential and necessary, it appears to be an undecidable in the technical sense of deconstructive terminology. On the one hand compassion is ruled out as pathological by the authority of reason; either because it is an evil which must not be engaged with nor unnecessarily multiplied, like in the case of a friend's suffering, which can only be 'endured without complaint' if need be; or because it would have to be classified as 'superfluous enjoyment' from which one must 'abstain', like—the example is Kant's—the "offensive variety of this compassion called mercy, by which is meant that kind of benevolence shown to the unworthy" which only serves to "boast" one's own "worthiness to be happy" (Kant 1886, p. 276).[20] As a merely 'added' extra, compassion seems to add nothing really necessary to the good will, which is self-sufficient from the moral point of view. In any case, as Kant emphasizes, one just cannot be obliged to be compassionate, just like "love", being a natural "affection", simply, i. e. naturally, "cannot be commanded" (Kant 1889, p. 15)—even though as far as "love" is concerned, it may actually appear as an almost "indispensable complement" to the moral *Pflichtvorstellung's* "command of duty", given that "the latter as an incentive, without the contribution of the former [i. e.: of love], is not very much to be counted on", as Kant concedes in *The end of all things* (Kant 2007, 08: 338; Kant 2001c, p. 230). On the other hand and 'practically' speaking, this added surrogate seems to be essential, at least in those particular cases in which compassion incites reason to leave its abstract 'representation of duty

[20] Translation modified.

on its own' and to not only will but to also act according to the categorical imperative. Thence for Kant it becomes an 'indirect duty' not to foreclose on the real life occasions in which compassion can possibly affect or rather infect the moral agent, driving him towards its cultivation.

From this it follows that, paradoxically, compassion is both on either side and beyond the Stoic dichotomy 'bear and forbear' to which Kant refers. It is not really contained by that dichotomy, neither logically nor 'practically'; and in case compassion should be contained, it gets excluded from 'practical' reason, at least theoretically. Conversely, insofar as compassion should be beyond this dichotomy, it gets nevertheless included into 'practical' reason, needed as it is to incite to effective action in exceptional cases. So, paradoxically, it is both excluded and included within 'practical', i. e. moral reason. Its logic can thus be reconstructed as follows: Kant's concept of moral subjectivity firstly excludes compassion, namely either as a pathological object of the will or 'as commanded'; yet it is precisely in this excluded compassion where the subject, secondly, rediscovers a therewith excluded part of itself; hence it thirdly and laboriously undertakes to recover this part by saving compassion in the form of cultivated (albeit 'painful') sympathy (which is not a duty but which not to avoid is an 'indirect duty'). Here one can see how Kant's concept of moral subjectivity becomes quite twisted as it seeks to save not the appearances but, so to speak, the *noumena*. "The subject is, as it were, internally excluded from its object [*en exclusion interne à son objet*]" (Lacan 2006b, p. 731), as can be stated here with Lacan. Compassion marks the inner outland of the subject, subjected as it is to an allegedly purely rational moral law. And it is through cultivated compassion that the subject's apathy, its disposition to will and act morally, i. e. humbly and respectfully at the same time, entertains an encrypted, i. e. encapsulated and hardly decipherable, communication with the pathological feelings of the social other—and eventually with his or her own pathological feelings, as it would be in the case of compassion with oneself, i. e. of self-pity, a concept which, not surprisingly, is alien to Kant's corpus.

So if for some moment Kant may have appeared to dismiss any form of pathological feeling as supplementary to intellectual reason alone (by the way quite similar to Plato's Socrates who e. g. in the *Republic*[21] dismisses even the artistically staged feelings of tragedy and comedy), then it must now be clear that some rhetorical dismissals notwithstanding Kant straightforwardly accepts a more or less cultivated compassion as a natural supplement to moral reason. Making solitary reason leave its purely intellectual, i. e. unpractical (if not immoral) abstractions, truly humane and thus virtuously charitable compassion is attending, *"theilnehmend"* (Kant 2007, 06: 456), but not properly communicative, *"mittheilend"* (ibid.: 457). Thus it comes close to—but is not identical with—the communicable, *mitteilbar* aesthetic feeling of the *Critique of Judgement*.

3. Morality and its Discontents

All things considered, compassion, *Mitleiden(schaft)*, remains a problematical feeling in Kant's late theory of moral virtue, whether principally or only factually, already because it will not always be possible to critically distinguish between natural and cultivated compassion; nor between cultivated compassion and 'boasting mercy'; moreover, and more importantly, because in order to properly function as a supplement to reason, cultivated compassion is contingent upon the repression of the

[21] Cf. e. g. Rep. 413a; 429c–d; 606a ff.

double of the feeling of respect, *Achtung*, namely upon the repression of the ominous 'pleasure in the law itself'. This is because it is precisely with cultivated compassion that Kant gets disquietingly close to such a commanded pleasure. Certainly, for Kant there simply is not anything like a commanded pleasure—the feeling of *Achtung* notwithstanding, as it is supposed to be not a 'pleasure in the law itself' but a pleasure on the mere occasion of that law; and the same would apply to the "moral pleasure (*moralischen Lust*)" or "moral enjoyment (*moralischen Genuss*)" which, as to Kant's Metaphysics, may be the "reward" (Kant 1886, p. 207; Kant 2007, 06: 391) of virtuously charitable actions.

Yet at closer inspection Kant's scattered remarks on the ominous topic of a 'pleasure in the law itself' and on a possibly 'commanded' feeling appear quite contradictory: On the one hand it must remain true for Kant that 'any determination of the will' is a 'feeling of pleasure'.[22] And the prime case for such a determination of the will, namely the will's determination by the moral law and the concomitant feeling of *Achtung*, is something which even forces itself upon us, *"sich für sich selbst uns aufdringt"*[23] (Kant 2007, 05: 031).[24] So remarkably, *Achtung* results as a 'moral pleasure' which the moral law forces upon us. However it is supposed to be no 'pleasure in the law itself'. On the other hand, Kant asserts in a footnote to his discussion of the sources of the aesthetic feeling in the *Critique of Judgement* that "[a]n obligation to enjoyment is a manifest absurdity [*Eine Verbindlichkeit zum Genießen ist eine offenbare Ungereimtheit*]." And he continues: "Thus the obligation to all actions

[22] Cf. Kant 2007, 06: 211; 05: 178.

[23] Kant's wording here is interesting: In the strictest sense the moral law not just forces itself upon us, but it "forces itself for itself [*sich für sich selbst*] upon us", as if this force would act on behalf of itself, like another subject, and not on behalf of e. g. a desired outcome, namely the subjectivation of the thus moralized individual.

[24] Cf. Kant 2007, 06: 036.

which have merely enjoyment for their aim can only be a pretended one; however spiritually it may be conceived (or decked out), even if it is a mystical, or so-called heavenly, enjoyment." (Kant 1914, p. 52 Fn. 2; Kant 2007, 05: 209, Fn. *) So whereas the moral law obliges the subject to the painful humiliation of its self resulting in the 'moral pleasure' of *Achtung*, it nevertheless does not oblige, it cannot oblige according to Kant, to enjoy pathologically, because that would be, according to this marginal assertion, manifestly absurd from a logical point of view. There is a similar argument in a passage from the Vigilantius-notes. There one can read that 'to enjoy having duties' would be 'contrary to the nature of duty' ('nature' here metaphorically in the sense of essence and not of physical quality). And one can paraphrase Kant in that passage by saying that to enjoy duties would be symptomatic of 'impulses' standing under the inacceptable 'authority' of 'painful or despotic commands':

> [...] it is also certain that every obligation is forthwith associated with a moral constraint, and that it is contrary to the nature of duty to *enjoy* having duties incumbent upon one; it is necessary, rather, that man's impulses should make him disinclined to fulfill the moral laws, and that these impulses should be overcome only through the authority of the latter, without it being possible to say that these laws demand respect in the manner of painful or despotic commands" (Kant 2001b, p. 259).[25]

Now to enjoy one's submission to a prohibitory law and to take this culpable enjoyment as a libidinally "regressive surrogate [*regressiver Ersatz*]" (Freud 1973, p. 240) for the enjoyment of the object prohibited by that law is exemplary for the "essence of masochism" (ibid., p. 241) as perversion according to Sigmund Freud's seminal text *A Child is Being Beaten*. So obviously what Kant excludes as a double of *Achtung*, throughout all these contradictory statements on the topic of a forced enjoyment, and without really getting at it, is something similar to what moral masochism is for Freud: pleasure in the law itself. As far as Freudian psychoanalysis is concerned, it

[25] Cf. Baxley 2015, p. 237.

identifies perversion as one of the major clinical structures besides neurosis/hysteria and psychosis. In Lacanian psychoanalytical theory, these structures represent the possible avatars *(Schicksale)* of the drives *(Triebe)* deriving from the castration complex. As such they represent different ways to cope with a primally repressed "pernicious enjoyment" (Lacan 1991, p. 52) which is the necessary libidinal remainder resulting from the institution of the super-ego *(Über-Ich)* as inner agent and executor of the moral law within the individual, i. e. from the individual's subjectivation. Thereby, as Freud explains in *Civilization and its Discontents (Das Unbehagen in der Kultur)*, morality is based on a self-sustaining and indeed self-aggravating libido-economic logic: The super-ego parasitically feeds on the pathological satisfaction which it itself prohibits. The super-ego derives its strength from the libidinal energy of what it prohibits. And so what Kant admitted as pathological 'surrogate' of moral reason, namely compassion (if only it is 'not commanded' but 'cultivated'), reveals itself as a quite *unbehaglich*, discontentful constituent of morality, namely in the form of an apriori compassion-*of*-oneself (rather than *with*-oneself), imposed as it always already is by the social other. So from a Freudian perspective, Kant's 'strength of reason' is in pathological deficit right from the start. The more pathological satisfaction the super-ego prohibits, however, the stronger it gets, and the stronger it gets, the more it prohibits, and so on. Now to conceive of how this spiral logic is set into motion, one must logically presuppose, firstly, a primordial moment in which the moral law would have been originally imposed, that is forced upon the subject, and, secondly, a concomitant primordially prohibited enjoyment. This is the enjoyment of a pathological object whose only function it would be to serve the institution of this prohibitory law. The concomitant state of mind would be identical with the determination of the will by that law.

In contradistinction to simple pleasure, Lacan at one point starts to reserve the term *"jouissance"* (Lacan 1967, 30.05.67, p. 274f.) for this enjoyment insofar as it is logically, ethically and aesthetically 'extimate' (included/excluded) to a subjectivity thence twisted by this extimacy.[26] And Lacan ranges the literary work of Kant's contemporary Marquis de Sade among the ancient ethical traditions in philosophy, e. g. Stoicism or Peripateticism, insofar as it would provide a noteworthy access to the experience of this enjoyment. (Lacan 2006a, p. 645) According to Freudian and Lacanian psychoanalysis some of antiquity's ethical schools, just like various Christian virtue doctrines, ultimately projected this enjoyment onto a Supreme Being, onto a fatherlike, almighty God, onto an Other who is the, as it were, Subject Supposed to Enjoy. As to Lacan, de Sade's *La philosophie dans le boudoir* supplements Kant's *Critique of practical reason* with its "truth" (ibid., p. 646)—and we should add: a truth about the enjoyment of this supreme Other which for Lacan turns out to be the unconscious as the discourse to which the subject is subjected. In a similar vein, Julia Kristeva speaks of a "logic of the intimate" which would work the Kantian 'practical' reason from within and which the literary work of de Sade would "stage [...] by illustrating how the intimate of the passionate and sensitive soul, because it finds itself under the empire of judging Reason and his de-sensitizing and unifying power, is an intimate which is *condemned to enjoy* this force"[27] (Kristeva 1997, p. 76).

It is with his theorem about the radical "propensity [*Hang*]" to do evil in *Religion within the Boundaries of Mere Reason* that Kant had earlier approached this 'pleasure

26 In the context of his concept of the Thing (la Chose) Lacan speaks of an intimate exteriority (*"extériorité intime"*) and of extimity (*"extimité"*) (Lacan 1986, p. 167).

27 My translation.

in the law itself' (Kant 2007, 07: 265).[28] Besides, with respect to the provocations in de Sade's writings one might want to follow Lacan's text on *Kant with Sade* and argue that Kant's theory of evil can actually come to terms with de Sade, given that de Sade's work would stay within an (anti-)virtue-ethical framework. As to Lacan, "[h]is [de Sade's] apology for crime merely impels him to an oblique acceptance of the Law. The Supreme Being is restored in Evil Action [*le Maléfice*]" (Lacan 2006a, p. 667). As far as Kant's *Religion* is concerned, it is the subject's "free power of choice [*freien Willkür*]" from which "depravity [*Bösartigkeit*]", which can also be called "perversity [*Verkehrtheit*] *(perversitas)*" (Kant 1996b, p. 83; Kant 2007, 06: 037), ultimately derives—depravity respectively perversity to be understood not as the simple propensity to yield to one's natural inclinations but as the formal "propensity of the power of choice [*Willkür*] to maxims that subordinate the incentives of the moral law to others (not moral ones)" (Kant 1996b, p. 78; Kant 2007, 06: 030). As a somewhat paradoxical "*innate* guilt [*angeborene Schuld*]" perversity "must nonetheless have originated from freedom [*aus der Freiheit entsprungen*]" (Kant 1996b, p. 84; Kant 2007, 06: 038). For Kant there is "no conceivable ground for us, therefore, from which moral evil could first have come in us [*kein begreiflicher Grund da, woher das moralische Böse in uns zuerst gekommen sein könne*]" (Kant 1996b, p. 88; Kant 2007, 06: 043).

And even though "the concept of freedom [...] first and foremost derives from this law", i. e. from the moral law as freedom's *ratio cognoscendi*, i. e. even though "the concept of the freedom of the power of choice [*der Begriff der Freiheit der Willkür*] does not precede in us the consciousness of the moral law but is only inferred

[28] Cf. Zac 1972, p. 153.

from the determinability of our power of choice through this law as unconditional command" (Kant 1996b, p. 93 Fn. *; Kant 2007, 06: 049), this for Kant cannot mean that "the freedom of the power of choice", *"Freiheit der Willkür"*, and thus evil would also be ontologically grounded in the consciousness of the moral law (as its *ratio essendi*).

Consequently, and given that for Kant there just cannot be a 'pleasure in the law itself', there can be no pleasure in the opposition to the law itself either. Hence there can be no "evil reason [*boshafte Vernunft*]" in which "resistance to the law would itself be thereby elevated to incentive [*Triebfeder*] (for without any incentive the power of choice cannot be determined)". This is because in being "so the subject would be made a *diabolical* being" which according to Kant "is however not applicable to the human being" (Kant 1996b, p. 82; Kant 2007, 06: 035).

4. The Aesthetics of Rationalization: Disgust, Boredom and Humour

As Kant thus ignores or rather pushes aside the possibility of perverse enjoyment within morality, he accordingly misjudges "[…] the *aesthetic* constitution [*ästhetische Beschaffenheit*], the *temperament* so to speak *of virtue*", too, conceiving of it as a "joyous frame of mind [*fröhliche Gemüthsstimmung*]", a "heart joyous in the compliance with its duty (not just complacency [*Behaglichkeit*] in the recognition of it)" (Kant 1996b, p. 73 Fn. †; Kant 2007, 06: 023 Fn. †)[29]. Kant detects, it is true, something "very ambiguous", i. e. some moral ambiguity within "the self-torment of a remorseful sinner". But this turns out to be unproblematic because it "usually [is] only an inward reproach for having offended against prudence" (ibid.). It is the usual self-

[29] Cf. Zac 1972, p. 147.

reproach of the offender for not having been clever enough (since he got caught). This is obviously not a moral disposition betraying a secret perverse enjoyment. And so for Kant this just fits all too well with a "slavish frame of mind [*sklavische Gemüthsstimmung*]" of those who, rather unambiguously, are just "weighed-down by fear and dejected" and likewise "never [...] without a hidden *hatred* of the law [*nie ohne einen verborgenenen Haß des Gesetzes*]" (ibid.) to which they feel themselves subjected. To this analysis of Kant one would have to object today with Lacan that at least in the case of masochism "the masochist is not" a mere "slave [*esclave*]" of the law (Lacan 1967, 30.05.67, p. 276f.).[30] Nor is it that the 'slavish frame of mind' would boil down to the simple question of being clever enough or not. Rather, such a mindset reveals the subject—the subject of the unconscious—as being more than just clever. The masochistic subject of the unconscious is all-too-clever, a clever-clever "old fox [*un petit malin*]" (ibid.) according to Lacan, since it is precisely in the act of submitting to the law and its punishment that he or she finds enjoyment. As Lacan states: "the masochist knows that he is within enjoyment [*le masochiste sait qu'il est dans la jouissance*]" (ibid.).

Be this as it may, Kant's *Critique of practical reason* sides with the derided "Stoic" who refuses to recognize anything evil in some "paroxysms of gout" which to him must appear as a merely physical pain:

> A bad thing [*Übel*] it certainly was, and his cry betrayed that; but that any evil [*ein Böses*] attached to him thereby, this he had no reason whatever to admit, for pain did not in the least diminish the worth of his person, but only that of his condition. If he had been conscious of a single lie it would have lowered his pride, but pain served only to elevate him [*ihn zu erheben*], when he was conscious that he had not deserved it by any unrighteous action by which he had rendered himself worthy of punishment. (Kant 1889, p. 151f.; Kant 2007, 05: 060)[31]

30 My translation.

31 Translation modified.

In contrast to the Stoics who moralized the whole of physical reality, Kant is surely more than critical of the tendency of "human reason [...] to link the course of nature with the laws of morality [*den Lauf der Natur an die Gesetze der Moralität anzuknüpfen*]" (Kant 1996b 114 Fn. *; Kant 2007, 06: 073 Fn. *).[32] Correspondingly, he makes a sharp distinction between the spheres of morality and of physical reality, i. e. pathology. Still for Kant these two extremes, the Stoic's cosmotheistic and his own quasi-monotheistic view, converge in the idea of an ideal elevation, *Erhebung*, a genuinely "moral apathy, *moralische Apathie*" which would be cleansed of all pathological activity ('lies', punishable 'unrighteous actions', etc.) as much as of all pathological passivity ("bluntness, *Fühllosigkeit*", "listlessness, *subjective Gleichgültigkeit*" and "indifference, *Indifferenz*" (Kant 1886, p. 226; Kant 2007, 06: 408)).[33]Aesthetically, Kant's 'moral apathy' should thus be free of the boredom (*Langeweile*) which characterizes, according to Hegel's *Phenomenology of Spirit*, the "general terms beyond which Stoicism cannot get", for instance "[t]he True and the Good, wisdom and virtue". For Hegel, these Stoic terms are "lacking the fullness of life"; they are "no doubt elevating [*erhebend*], but since they cannot in fact produce any expansion of the content, they soon become boring [*fangen sie bald an, Langeweile zu machen*]" (Hegel 1977, p. 122).[34]

32 On Kant and Stoicism cf. Schneewind 1996, 292ff., particularly p. 294. Cf. also Santozki 2006, p. 508, who argues that despite many parallels Kant's critical philosophy was developed without substantial recourse to ancient Stoicism: *"Wenn man ihn [Kant] überhaupt in eine antike Richtung einordnen kann, dann ist die Stoa zu nennen. Er selbst hätte sich als kritischer Philosoph allerdings sicher gegen derartige Zuschreibungen gewehrt. [...] Negativ konnte der Gang durch die drei Kritiken jeweils begründet zeigen, dass eine genuine Auseinandersetzung mit der Antike für die Genese der grundlegenden Prämissen der jeweiligen Theorien keine Rolle spielt."*

33 Translation modified. Cf. Assmann 2003, passim, for the distinction between monotheism and cosmotheism.

34 Translation modified.

Against this background it must have been unthinkable for Kant that the pain-trodden's sage elevation, *Erhebung*, might secretly contain a malign (i. e. all-too-cleverly evil) pleasure as an added extra, as a pernicious surplus enjoyment, for instance a kind of elevated self-pity. But then how would Kant have judged the legendary apathetic self-contentment of the Stoic "[…] Epictetus who, when his master was twisting his leg, said, smiling and unmoved, 'You will break my leg', and when it was broken, he added, 'Did I not tell you that you would break it?'" (Origen 2001, chap. LIII). Is not Epictetus' jovial countenance in face of a pain unjustly suffered an extreme form of what Kant had in mind when he praised "contentment *(acquiescentia)*" as an "enjoyment analogous to the self-sufficiency which we can ascribe only to the Supreme Being" in the *Critique of Practical Reason*?[35] Actually, it is not. For Kant sees a limit to moral elevation beyond which man's "moral capacity" becomes "fancifully" exaggerated and thus "nonsense" (Kant 2001a, p. 32). And it is precisely some famous Stoics which Kant—as quoted by Herder—has in mind here: "Seneca was an impostor, Epictetus strange and fanciful." (Ibid.)[36] However, can Kant's moral apathy, the subject's countenance, based as it is on reason's practical law only and on a solitary *Pflichtvorstellung* ('representation of duty on its own'), be said to be free of all fancies?

---

[35] See above (Kant 1889, p. 215).

[36] Schneewind 1996, p. 292 quotes the whole passage from which this phrase is taken: "Man fancifully exaggerates his moral capacity and sets before himself the most perfect goodness; the outcome is nonsense; but what is required of us? The Stoic's answer: I shall raise myself above myself, … rise superior to my own afflictions and needs, and with all my might be good, be the image of godhood. But how so, for godhood has no obligations, yet you certainly do… Now the god departs and we are left with man, a poor creature, loaded with obligations. Seneca was an impostor, Epictetus strange and fanciful" (Cf. Kant 2001a, p. 32). Schneewind resumes Kant's relationship to Stoicism as follows: "Kant's reservations about Stoicism were as pervasive as his appreciation of it" (ibid.).

Interestingly, for Freud's *Psychopathology of Everyday Life* section on *Erroneously carried out actions*, it is precisely the "striking countenance [*Fassung*] which the patients show" in the face of "apparently accidental injuries" which "in the more serious cases of psychoneuroses" may "betray the portion of unconscious intention" causally involved therein. An analysis of the respective unconscious intention regularly reveals that these "pretended accidents" in truth "are really self-inflicted" and "symptoms of the disease". Behind the seeming "calmness, *Ruhe*" we must, according to Freud, suppose an unconscious and "constantly lurking tendency to self-punishment [...] which skilfully, makes use of an external situation" (Freud 1922, p. 198f.).[37] This self-punishment results in a pernicious enjoyment through which the subject (of the unconscious) communicates with itself. Freud's exemplary case in the *Psychopathology* is a young married woman who

> [...] broke her leg below the knee in a carriage accident so that she was bedridden for weeks. The striking part of it was the lack of any manifestation of pain and the calmness [*Ruhe*] with which she bore her misfortune. This calamity ushered in a long and serious neurotic illness, from which she was finally cured by psychotherapy. During the treatment I discovered the circumstances surrounding the accident, as well as certain impressions which preceded it. The young woman with her jealous husband spent some time on the farm of her married sister, in company with her numerous other brothers and sisters with their wives and husbands. One evening she gave an exhibition of one of her talents before this intimate circle; she danced artistically the 'cancan', to the great delight of her relatives, but to the great annoyance of her husband, who afterward whispered to her, 'Again you have behaved like a prostitute'. The words took effect; we will leave it undecided whether it was just on account of the dance. That night she was restless [*unruhig*] in her sleep, and the next forenoon she decided to go out driving. She chose the horses herself, refusing one team and demanding another. Her youngest sister wished to have her baby with its nurse accompany her, but she opposed this vehemently. During the drive she was nervous; she reminded the coachman that the horses were getting skittish, and as the fidgety [*unruhigen*] animals really produced a momentary difficulty she jumped from the carriage in fright and broke her leg, while those remaining, in the carriage were uninjured. Although after the disclosure of these details we can hardly doubt that this accident was really contrived, we cannot fail to admire the skill which forced the accident to mete out a punishment so suitable to the crime. For as it happened 'cancan' dancing with her became impossible for a long time" (ibid., p. 199f.).

[37] Translation modified.

Here self-communication adopts the twisted form of an acting out of an unconscious phantasy of self-punishment. It is rooted in what can be called a symptomatic 'compassion-of-oneself'. "[I]n our present state of civilization", writes Freud in 1904, "[t]he self-inflicted injury which does not entirely tend toward self-annihilation has [...] no other choice [...] than to hide itself behind the accidental [...]. Formerly, it was a customary sign of mourning, at other times it expressed itself in ideas of piety [*Frömmigkeit*] and renunciation of the world [*Weltentsagung*]." (Ibid., p. 199 Fn. 1)

It is known, of course, how Kant repeatedly denounces *Schwärmerei* and other ambiguous forms of moral pathology like e. g. bigotry. And it has been evidenced above how much Kant's moral subject is supposed to differ from that through its 'joyous frame of mind' etc. Yet in Kant's later philosophy traces of a symptomatic enjoyment at the roots of moral subjectivity can be detected, too. A comparison with de Sade is helpful here, following Lacan's text on *Kant with Sade*, for it suggests that the elevated and self-content enjoyment of the virtuous subject would turn into, so to speak, 'moral' disgust under de Sadean conditions: "Imagine a revival of Epictetus in Sadean experience: 'You see, you broke it', he says, pointing to his leg. To reduce *jouissance* to the misery of an effect in which one's quest stumbles—doesn't this transform it into disgust?" (Lacan 2006a, p. 651) And as Jacques Derrida suggests in *Economimesis*, "the experience of disgust" together with "the scheme of vomiting" (Derrida 1981, p. 21) mark the blind spot of Kant's rationalistic moralism. Or rather it occupies "[...] within the Kantian system a strategic point that unites all faculties", as Winfried Menninghaus convincingly argues (Menninghaus 2003, p. 114).[38] It is in Kant's own conception of disgust indeed where his contradictory statements on the paradoxical topic of a 'commanded feeling', a 'pleasure in the law itself' or an 'enjoyment of duties' converge—statements like: that the determination of the will by the moral law 'imposes itself (*sich aufdringt*)' and that *Achtung* is the 'moral pleasure' resulting from this imposition; that it is 'contrary to the nature of duty to *enjoy* having duties incumbent upon one'; that 'an obligation to enjoyment is a manifest absurdity', just like it 'cannot be commanded' to have a certain 'affection' like e. g. 'love'.

This is not least because disgust (including possible variants) is the only form of forced enjoyment that Kant openly admits (again *Achtung* and its reverse, humiliation, notwithstanding). In the *Critique of Judgement*, § 48 dealing with the *Relation of Genius to Taste*, Kant defines disgust, *Ekel*, as the "[...] peculiar sensation, which rests on mere imagination, [in which] the object is represented as [if] it were imposing itself for our enjoyment [*als ob er sich zum Genusse aufdränge*] while we strive against it with all our might" (Kant 1914, p. 195; Kant 2007, 05: 312).[39] As it were, disgust is a feeling which commands itself to us. The aesthetic result according to Kant is that in disgust, *Ekel*, "the artistic representation of the object is no longer distinguished from the nature of the object itself in our sensation", which is to say that an imaginary let alone symbolic distancing of the object is impossible. Thus disgust is the singular "kind of ugliness which cannot be represented in accordance

[38] On Kant's concept of disgust cf. Menninghaus 2003, particularly pp. 103–120. Menninghaus observes that „[t]he sensation of disgust judges, as it were, on physical, aesthetic, and moral levels, thus occupying—very much like the sensation of beauty—within the Kantian system a strategic point that unites all faculties. It supplements the purely theoretical critique with a test of taste—with a dietetic organon judging all sorts of 'food for the intellect'." (Ibid., p. 114f.)

[39] Translation modified.

with nature". It cannot be forborn because it cuts through any kind of imaginary or symbolic distancing. Disgust is a formation of the 'real' in Lacan's sense. Therefore it ruins ("*zu Grunde zu richten*") "all aesthetical satisfaction [*ästhetische Wohlgefallen*] and consequently artificial beauty [*Kunstschönheit*]" (ibid.). As disgust collapses the difference between sensation and representation, it also tends to collapse the difference between the subject and the disgustful object—be it a suffering human being. From an aesthetical point of view, it thus marks the blind spot of the ethically and logically necessary self-implication of the morally judging subject into his own systematized rationalizations. Through disgust, the moral subject is blinded and thus beyond good and evil. Yet at the same time, we may presume, disgust is just the extreme reverse side of compassion and thus is related to the very possibility of practical reason; as surrogate or supplement of morality's truth, it kicks the solitary *Pflichtvorstellung* into the fullness of life. Moreover, we can conclude that in analogy to the feeling of *Achtung*, which is a feeling "the necessity of which we can discern (*einsehen*)", in the case of disgust it is necessity as such, i. e. the necessity of subjectivation, i. e. morality's *ultima ratio*, which becomes an object of aesthetic experience. Thus it appears that in Kant's moral philosophy disgust is the—ugly—truth of the "necessity, indeed urgency" of "a demand of morality itself", namely of "finding a sensible representation of morality" (Guyer 1993, p. 178).[40]

---

[40] Cf. Menninghaus: "While virtually all pertinent scholarly work on Kant focuses on the duality of the sublime and the beautiful, the Kantian system is in fact distinguished by a triad—that of 'the feelings of the sublime, the beautiful, and the disgusting'. This triad proves to be highly functional with regard to the paradigm of philosophical organa. [...] The beautiful and sublime positively compensate for theoretical deficits of foundation and practical deficits of motivation; the feeling of disgust warns us away, and shelters us in negative-apotropaic fashion, from giving in to what would be opposite to the (groundless) good or the (unknowable) purposiveness of nature. As an effect of cultivation, such desirable achievements do not constitue a miraculous natural phenomenon, proving that the human being is naturally good in essence. Rather, to speak with Freud, in the end these positive functions of disgust are instituted by the superego" (Menninghaus 2003, p. 116).

Aesthetically speaking again, this ultimate necessity appears here in a most 'accidental' (Freud) form, namely in a form which, in everyday experience, is as pervasive as it is unpredictable: boredom. And just as disgust is the reverse side of compassion, *Mitleid*, and by the same token the discontentful double of respect, *Achtung*, so analogously is boredom the discontentful (*unbehaglich*) double of Kant's moral apathy. For it is "disgust" that, in Kant's *Anthropology*, essentially defines "boredom". Boredom, *lange Weile*, writes Kant, boils down to disgust or nausea, given that boredom is the "disgust [*Anekelung*] with one's own existence, which arises when the mind is empty of the sensations toward which it incessantly strives [*aus der Leerheit des Gemüths an Empfindungen, zu denen es unaufhörlich strebt, der langen Weile*]" (Kant 2006, p. 43; Kant 2007, 07: 152). In other words: boredom is the disgust, *Ekel*, felt on the occasion of a permanently frustrated striving for sensations. As we have every reason to suspect here, boredom or disgust become morally relevant precisely in cases where the 'representation of duty on its own', emptied as it is of all 'pathological' determinations, would not accomplish the practical determination of the will.

So we can further presume that it is through the aesthetical (i. e. ultimately: pathological) feelings of disgust and/or boredom that "[t]he rule of the Judgement according to laws of pure practical reason" (i. e. the categorical imperative) can indeed get suspended, a rule which obliges to "ask yourself whether, if the action you propose were to take place by a law of the system of nature of which you were yourself a part, you could regard it as possible by your own will. Everyone does, in fact, decide by this rule whether actions are morally good or evil" (Kant 1889, p. 161; Kant 2007, 05: 069). Affected by disgust/boredom, the Kantian subject, like the Stoic, simply cannot ask him- or herself whether he or she 'could regard' the proposed action 'as possible by his or her own will'[41]. This is because it is precisely disgust/boredom which masks both the self-implication of the subject's will into the moral law (conceived of in analogy to a 'system of nature') and the unconscious (quasi-natural, quasi-pathological) "pre-determinism" of the will resulting from it; how such pre-determinism could possibly "co-exist with freedom" is something which, as to Kant's *Religion*, "we want to discern [*einsehen*], but we never shall" (Kant 2006, p. 94, Fn. *; Kant 2007, 06: 049).

It cannot be discerned, in any case, unless the subject stops ignoring his or her as it were 'moral' disgust, which is compassion in its most extreme, namely its most debased form. If, as Kant claims, in disgust 'the artistic representation of the object is no longer distinguished from the nature of the object itself in our sensation', i. e. if not even the artistic representation can temper disgust, then a *fortiori* we may conclude that actually any representation of the (disgusting) object 'is no longer distinguished from the nature of the object itself in our sensation'. Such 'moral' disgust thus makes it impossible to decide whether a sympathetic affect springs from intuition or rather from reason, i. e. whether from 'pathological' infection by a social other ('*humanitas aesthetica*') or rather from the subject's 'practical' free will ('*humanitas practica*'). Thus in the experience of disgust the subject can no longer decide whether its 'representation of duty', *Pflichtvorstellung*, is 'pathological' or 'practical'. For it is only in pure "thinking" that I can imagine that "I am *free*, because I am not in an other, but remain simply and solely in communion with myself [*schlechthin bei mir selbst bleibe*], [...]"; nothing but "[...] my activity in conceptual thinking is a movement within myself [*meine Bewegung in Begriffen ist eine Bewegung in mir selbst*]",

[41] Cf. Cooper 1996, p. 266.

as Hegel remarks in the *Phenomenology* with respect to (not only) ancient Stoicism. As Hegel explains, this is because "[...] in the case of a representation [*Vorstellung*], [...] consciousness still has specially to bear in mind that this is its representation [*Vorstellung*]; on the contrary, the concept [*Begriff*] is for me straightaway my concept [*Begriff*]" (Hegel 1977, p. 120).[42] Disgust breaks up this rational self-communion. So besides veiling the self-implication of the moral subject into its object and besides blurring the distinction between pathological and moral compassion, disgust lastly makes it impossible even to discern whether the *Pflichtvorstellung* really is the subject's very own representation or not, and whether it is a representation of a concept or a representation in the sensuous, aesthetic sense.

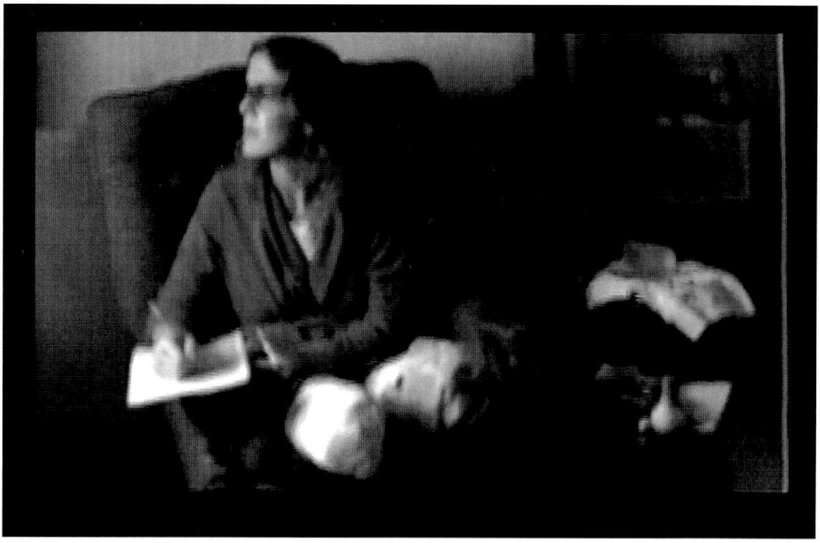

Screenshot from *The Amputee* (1974) directed by David Lynch

42 Translation modified.

While the *Pflichtvorstellung* tends to become indiscernible in the experience of disgust, and despite Kant's verdict about the impossible artification of disgustful objects, there are nevertheless artistic strategies to counter the symptomatic knot interlacing disgust, apathetic boredom and painful compassion. David Lynch's *The Amputee* of 1974 artistically stages and exposes such symptomatic feelings as they eventually mask an unconscious over-determination. The objective humor involved in Lynch's short film communicates something unfathomable which cannot be discerned, it is true, but which can be enjoyed and thus sensed.

References

Baxley, A. M. 2015, "Virtue, self-mastery and the autocracy of practical reason" in: L. Denis et al., *Kant's Lectures on Ethics. A critical guide*, Cambridge University Press, Cambridge, pp. 223–238.

Borges, M 2008, "Physiology and the Controlling of Affects in Kant's Philosophy" in: *Kantian review*, Vol. 13, issue 2, pp. 46–66.

Cartwright, D. E. 1984, "Kant, Schopenhauer, and Nietzsche on the Morality of Pity" in: Journal of the History of Ideas, Vol. 45, No. 1 (Jan. – Mar., 1984), pp. 83–98.

Cooper, J. M. 1996, "Eudaimonism, the Appeal to Nature, and Moral Duty" in: S. Engstrom, and J. Whiting, *Aristotle, Kant and the Stoics,* Cambridge University Press, Cambridge, pp. 261–284.

Denis, L. 2000, "Kant's Cold Sage and the Sublimity of Apathy" in: L. Denis, *Kantian Review,* Vol. 4, University of Wales Press, Cardiff, pp. 48–73.

Derrida, J. 1981, "Economimesis" in: *Diacritics, The Ghost of Theology: Readings of Kant and Hegel*, Vol. 11, No. 2, pp. 2–25.

Fichte, J. G. 2013, *Grundlagen des Naturrechts,* Ausgewählte Werke in sechs Bänden. Zweiter Band, WBG, Darmstadt.

Freud, S. 1922, *Psychopathology of everyday life,* 9th edition. T. Fisher Unwin, London.

Freud, S. 1973, "Ein Kind wird geschlagen" in: *Zwang, Paranoia und Perversion. Freud-Studienausgabe,* Bd. 7. Hg. von Alexander Mitscherlich, Fischer, Frankfurt a. M., pp. 229–254.

Goy, I. 2007, "Immanuel Kant über das moralische Gefühl der Achtung" in: *Zeitschrift für philosophische Forschung*, Bd. 61, H. 3 (Jul.– Sep., 2007), pp. 337–360.

Guyer, P. 1996, *Kant and the experience of freedom essays on aesthetics and morality,* Cambridge Univ. Press, Cambridge.

Hegel, G. W. F., Miller, A. V. & Findlay J. N. 1977, *Phenomenology of spirit,* Oxford University Press, Oxford.

Honneth, A. 2001, "Die transzendentale Notwendigkeit von Intersubjektivität (Zweiter Lehrsatz: § 3)" in: J.-C. Merle, *Johann Gottlieb Fichte. Grundlage des Naturrechts,* Akademie-Verlag, Berlin, pp. 63–80.

Kant, I. 1886, *The metaphysic of ethics,* 3rd edition, T. & T. Clark, Edinburgh.

Kant, I. 1889, *Kant's Critique of Practical Reason and other Works on the Ethics,* Translated by Thomas Kingsmill Abbott, Longman's, London.

Kant, I. and Bernard, J. H. 1914, *Kant's Critique of Judgement,* 2nd edition, Macmillan Press, London.

Kant, I. 1996, "Religion within the boundaries of mere reason", in: Wood, di Giovanni: *Immanuel Kant. Religion and Rational Theology,* Cambridge University Press, Cambridge, pp. 39–216.

Kant, I. 2006, *Anthropology from a pragmatic point of view,* Cambridge University Press, Cambridge.

Kant, I. 2007, *Akademie-Ausgabe,* Universität Duisburg-Essen, Essen. Available from; <https://korpora.zim.uni-due.de/Kant/>. [10 January 2016]

Kant, I. 2001a, "Kant's practical philosophy: Herder's lecture notes (selections)" in: I. Kant & P. L. Heath, *Lectures on ethics,* Cambridge University Press., Cambridge, pp. 1–36.

Kant, I. 2001b. "Johann Friedrich Vigilantius: Notes on the lectures of Mr. Kant on the Metaphysics of Ethics" in: I. Kant & P. L. Heath, *Lectures on ethics,* Cambridge University Press., Cambridge, pp. 249–452.

Kant, I. 2001c, "The end of all things" in: I. Kant, *Religion and rational theology,* Cambridge University Press, Cambridge pp. 217–232.

Lacan, J. 1967, *Le Séminaire livre XIV: La logique du phantasme* (1966-67), Lacan-Archive, Bregenz.

Lacan, J. 1986, *Le Seminaire livre VII: L'Éthique de la psychanalyse* (1959-60), Seuil, Paris.

Lacan, J. 1991, *Le Séminaire XVII: L'envers de la psychoanalyse* (1969-70), Seuil, Paris.

Lacan, J. 2006a, "Kant with Sade" in *Écrits* [1966], Translated by Bruce Fink, Norton, New York/London, pp. 645–670.

Lacan, J. 2006b, "Science and truth" in *Écrits* [1966], Translated by Bruce Fink, Norton, New York/London, pp. 726–745.

Menninghaus, W. 2003, *Disgust. Theory and history of a strong sensation,* State University of New York Press, Albany.

Mieth, C. 2015, entry for "Liebe" in M. Willaschek et al., *Kant-Lexikon*, de Gruyter, Berlin/ Boston, pp. 1412–1414.

Molina, E. 2013, „Kant y el ideal del sabio", in: *ideas y valores,* Vol. LXII · suplemento n.o 1, pp. 171–183.

Origen 2001, *Contra Celsum*, chap. LIII. Available from: <http://www.earlychristianwritings.com/text/origen167>. [10 January 2016]

Wood, A 2015, "Kant's history of ethics" in L Denis et al. Kant's Lectures on Ethics: A critical guide, Cambridge University Press, Cambridge, pp. 120–137.

Zac, S 1972, "Kant, les stoïciens et le christianisme" in Revue de Métaphysique et de Morale, No. 2, pp. 137–165.

Filmography

The Amputee 1974, Lynch, D, [film], USA: Criterion Collection.

Literature and Health: Proust as Symptomatologist

2

Claudio Rozzoni

1. Literature Between Illness and Health

Marcel Proust was born on 10 July 1871 in Auteuil—a little village subsequently annexed to Paris. His father, Adrien Proust, 37 years old at the time, would go on to become a world-famous doctor.[1] For Marcel's father, his career would provide a veritable social advancement. From the very beginning of his brilliant medical career, Proust's father showed both a remarkable and profound scientific sensibility, as well as a strong devotion to his mission as a doctor.[2] Robert, the second-born son of Dr Adrien Proust, would go on to follow in his father's footsteps: considering that Robert would later become a surgeon, it is clear that he inherited from his famous parent the *côté médical*. Nevertheless, even though Marcel formally followed a different path, could we say that in a certain sense he did the same as his brother?

By looking at the very first pages, the *Recherche* reader will certainly notice how Marcel Proust has abundant recourse to metaphors referring to the medical world.[3] In particular, I would like to point out how Marcel seems to have inherited from his father a peculiar vision. A vision that can be called *clinical*. Jean-Yves Tadié also notes that in Proust's masterwork, "the subject of medicine is not present solely in

---

1 See Ferré 1959, p. 33.

2 See Ferré 1959, pp. 38–39. For a further discussion about the figure of Adrien Proust, see Bizub 2006.

3 Only to mention one of the first occurrences: "Nearly midnight. The hour when an invalid [*le malade*], who has been obliged to set out on a journey and to sleep in a strange hotel, awakened by a sudden spasm, sees with glad relief a streak of daylight showing under his door. Thank God, it is morning! [...] The ray of light beneath his door is extinguished. It is midnight [...] and he must lie all night in agony with no one to bring him relief" (Proust 1983a, p. 4). On the presence of the 'medical side' in Proust's masterwork see also Béhar 1993, Bizub 2006, Genin 1999 and Fraisse 2013, particularly chapter XV.

the characters, or in the illnesses that feature in" the novel. Rather, "Proust's view of the world, of life and its passions, was also medical: everything is a matter of pathology, of symptoms, and every description becomes a diagnosis, nowhere more so than where love is concerned" (Tadié 2000, p. 35).

Thus, on the one hand, we have Robert—Marcel's younger brother—who chose the same career as his father, while, on the other hand, we have Marcel who acquired—and, as we will see, developed—from the *côté paternel* a vision that, starting with the Deleuzian work we are going to refer to, we can characterize as that of the great *symptomatologist*. I am talking about a particular vision that, according to the French philosopher, is not something unnecessary that merely adds itself to the essence of the writer. It is rather an essential part of what he or she is. Indeed, for Gilles Deleuze, being a writer implies a particular relationship with illness and health. In his last book (*Essays Critical and Clinical*), Deleuze begins his preface by stating: "The problem of *writing*: writers, as Proust says, invent a new language within language, a foreign language, as it were. They bring to light new grammatical or syntactic powers. They force language outside its customary furrows, they make it *delirious* [*délirer*]" (Deleuze 1998, p. lv).

Following Deleuze, we can then suggest that there is something like a 'space of play' at the limit of language, a space in which language can derail from its accustomed paths. A "limit" that "is not outside language," but, rather "is the outside *of* language" (Deleuze 1998, p. lv). In fact, it is not a threshold merely referring to something that simply lies behind language. Instead, it is language itself that creates its outside, thereby "mak[ing] possible" a peculiar "*seeing*" and a peculiar "*hearing*" (Deleuze 1998, p. lv). On the one hand, Deleuze recalls how Samuel Beckett "spoke of 'drilling holes' in language in order to see or hear 'what was lurking behind'" and, more in general, he maintains that "one must say of every writer: he is a seer [*voyant*], a hearer, 'ill seen ill said,' she is a colorist, a musician" (Deleuze 1998, p. lv).[4] Yet, on the other hand, this "behind" is not to be thought of as a static state that is found merely by pulling aside the curtain of language. Deleuze is not trying to define a situation in which we would have, as it were, a silent truth hidden behind a linguistic veil.

Conversely, what is at stake in language's work with its own limits is the possibility to express the "events" *insisting*—as the Deleuze of *The Logic of Sense* would put it—at its surface. In this very context, then, on the one hand we can speak of a "*clinical state*" of language, where and when "words no longer open out onto anything" (Deleuze 1998, p. lv), and, on the other hand, of the healthy function of literature when—as we will see—it is able to open to *Life*. In such a case "Literature is a health" (Deleuze 1998, p. lv), even though that healthiness often implies a physical fragility: "In this respect artists are like philosophers. What little health they possess is often too fragile" (Deleuze & Guattari 1994, p. 172). Nevertheless, the very reason for such a frailty is not to be found in "their illnesses or neuroses," but exactly insofar as they have become *seers*: "they have seen something in life that is too much for anyone, too much for themselves, and that has put on them the quiet mark of death" (Deleuze & Guattari 1994, p. 172). Becoming a seer can entail the sacrifice of one's own empirical body.[5]

---

4 Recall that "being a seer" is a condition that for Deleuze does not pertain exclusively to the writer, but that can apply to the 'artist in general'. We need only to think, for example, to the characterization of the director as a seer in Cinema 2 (see Deleuze 1989, p. 126).

5 In this regard, see what Proust writes about the "terrible ravaged faces" of the "old Rembrandt" and "Beethoven": "let us accept the physical injury which is done to us for the sake of the spiritual knowledge which grief brings" (Proust 1983f., p. 944).

2. The Writer as Symptomatologist

In *Coldness and Cruelty*, we read:

> What are the uses of literature? The names of Sade and Masoch have been used to denote two basic perversions, and as such they are outstanding examples of the efficiency of literature. Illnesses are sometimes named after typical patients, but more often it is the doctor's name that is given to the disease (Roger's disease, Parkinson's disease, etc.). The principles behind this labeling deserve closer analysis. The doctor does not invent the illness, he dissociates symptoms that were previously grouped together, and links up others that were dissociated. In short he builds up a profoundly original clinical picture. [...] The history of symptomatology [...]: symptoms are named, renamed and regrouped in various ways. [...] Great clinicians are the greatest doctors: when a doctor gives his name to an illness this is a major linguistic and semiological step, inasmuch as a proper name is linked to a given group of signs, that is, *a proper name is made to connote signs* (Deleuze 1991, pp. 15–16).

That is what great *symptomatologists* can do. Nevertheless, it often happens that doctors themselves—who are strongly anchored to the paradigms through which they 'read' reality—remain blind to the unknown manifestations of illness. It is the *'great' sick individual*, however, who discovers new symptomatological contexts. According to Deleuze, Sade and Masoch are two perfect examples of convalescents who have shown themselves able to bring to light original symptomatological constellations. In Proust's masterwork an analogous situation is to be found. Let us take into consideration the most significant example in this sense, namely the description of the illness suffered by the narrator's grandmother, which brings her to death. The doctors who are called to deal with her sickness seem unable to recognize its actual behavior. Their diagnoses are always late and incapable of detecting the imperceptible progression of the illness. Every doctor, 'armed' with his own paradigm, tries to capture the unpredictable illness's behavior in his conceptual net. Though, in spite of every effort, such an outcome is never achieved.[6] Every time a new symptom emerges it exceeds the limits of the doctor's interpretative model and eludes their attempt at

[6] In this regard, consider also the behavior of "Professor E—" in Proust 1983d, p. 664, who, encountering the narrator a while after his grandmother's death, tries to ascertain whether or not she finally died of the "extremely grave" "prognosis" he formulated when he briefly visited the patient.

classification. Dr Cottard and Dr du Boulbon adopt exactly the same approach in trying to identify which illness afflicts the narrator's grandmother. The former resorts to a paradigm that can be defined as 'classic', whereas the latter follows a paradigm that can legitimately be called 'psychosomatic'. In any case, in the sickness that seizes the grandmother, both doctors can only recognize the illness they were already expecting to find, *a priori*, even before visiting the patient. But the disease in question still presents new ways of escaping these paradigms.

Nonetheless, throughout the novel it is the narrator who shows himself able to pick up on the pathological signs without reducing them to what he already knew. We could say that he developed an aptitude that one might define as phenomenological. It is true that Proust was familiar with many medical notions, of course. We know that he put his father's legacy to use in the creation of his protagonist: the narrator displays a very good knowledge of clinical classification and medical lexicon. Besides, in *À la recherche*, not only does he prove himself able to describe the manifestations of an illness but he also correlates the laws he sees in action in the developments of the sickness with those of reality *lato sensu*.

However, that being said, the narrator's eyes are not anchored to rigid paradigms influencing what he sees, leading him to see something that was already supposed to be found in the event he observed. He does not project his prejudices onto the *phenomena* that he experiences. For instance, he is able to read the 'behavior' of the illness through the signs expressed by the suffering body, bringing the description of these laws to a deeper level. He is able to hear the silent voice of the *stranger* that seems to invade his grandmother's body. It is precisely through this body that the *stranger*, usually invisible, can manifest itself:

> We make the acquaintance of the *Stranger* whom we hear coming and going in our brain. True, we do not know him by sight, but from the sounds we hear him regularly make we can form an idea of his habits. Is he a malefactor? One morning, we can no longer hear him. He has gone. Ah! if only it were for ever! In the evening he has returned. What are his plans? (Proust 1983c, p. 327, my italics).

It is worth recalling that at the end of the novel the narrator states that *Time* too—otherwise invisible—needs bodies to manifest itself, just like the *Stranger*. The narrator knows very well that regardless of the 'initial model' used to confront the signs of illness—the signs of a stranger—the model is fated to fail when facing unknown symptoms in a static way. If the paradigm is unable to change, the doctor will try in vain to reduce the sickness to its form. In *À la recherche* we see doctors at work, doctors who formulate diagnoses starting with preconceived schemata, to which they try to narrow down the sickness—the silent intruder—to both a familiar and reassuring form. Similarly, in the foreword to *Coldness and Cruelty,* Deleuze states that "sado-masochism is a syndrome that ought to be split up into irreducible causal chains," and, given that "the judgment of the clinician is prejudiced," "we need to go back to the beginning and read Sade and Masoch," thereby "tak[ing] an entirely different approach, the *literary approach*" (Deleuze 1991, p. 14). As we can deduce from this quotation, the emphasis is put on the side of the literary eye that can overcome the rigid frame of the clinical eye, often incapable of grasping the capricious behavior of the illnesses, and, more generally, the inscrutable connection between symptoms.

Of course, unfortunately, the narrator's descriptions in literature cannot heal more than other paradigms do—and probably less.[7] Deleuze clarifies that "symptomatology" is not "etiology" nor "therapeutics":

---

7 "For, medicine being a compendium of the successive and contradictory mistakes of medical practitioners, when we summon the wisest of them to our aid the chances are that we may be relying on a scientific truth the error of which will be recognised in a few years' time. So that to believe in medicine would be the height of folly, if not to believe in it were not a greater folly still, for from this mass of errors a few truths have in the long run emerged" (Proust, 1983c, pp. 308–309).

> Perhaps there are three different medical acts: symptomatology, or the study of signs; etiology, or the search for causes; and therapeutics, or the search for and application of a treatment. Whereas etiology and therapeutics are integral parts of medicine, symptomology appeals to a kind of neutral point, a limit that is premedical or sub-medical, belonging as much to art as to medicine: it's all about drawing a 'portrait'. The work of art exhibits symptoms, as do the body or the soul, albeit in a very different way. In this sense, the artist or writer can be a great symptomatologist, just like the best doctor: so it is with Sade or Masoch (Deleuze 2004, p. 132).[8]

The narrator's description of his grandmother's illness aims to survey the movement of the illness and to question it further. First of all, what the description shows is that illnesses are not static. Illnesses do not have definite and rigid boundaries, fixed once and for all. As we saw with Deleuze, the gesture that baptizes a sickness designates a "linguistic and semiological step," which "ties" together a set of symptoms that in the future could be disconnected or reconnected to other symptoms to form a new medical case. It is exactly *this* "medical act" that does not pertain exclusively to medicine. Indeed, as a "study of signs," its action reaches a "neutral" zone, a liminal one, which no longer refers solely to medicine but constitutes a "zero point" that is "located almost outside medicine [...] where artists and philosophers and doctors and patients can come together" (Deleuze 2004, p. 134).

As we have seen, this symptomatologist's sensitivity is an essential feature of the artist, of Proust the writer, and not a contingent quality that would enrich his vision. This clinical *côté* is a constitutive aspect of his style and allows his narrator to discover aspects in reality that would otherwise be invisible. In Proust's masterwork, each character is defined as such because he or she emits "signs," "symptoms" which are the points that resound one with another creating a constellation: a character is a constellation that—even if it is referred to by a proper name (Albertine, Charlus)—does not cease to relate to the differences that shape it.

---

8 Translation modified.

Now, it has to be clarified that these character-constellations are not simply discovered by the narrator. On the contrary, they are formed through a process animated by the manifestations of symptoms. Before being able to draw a constellation, the narrator's eyes as well as his understanding have to deal with *nebulas*. It will suffice here to mention, once again, the two great nebulas, galaxies [*nébuleuses*] that appear in *À l'ombre des jeunes filles en fleurs (Within a Budding Grove)*: Albertine—that is, some sparks indistinctly emerging from the galaxies of the "little band" of Balbec—and Charlus—namely a gaze enigmatically ruled by the inscrutable movement of "a pair of eyes."[9] In fact, they make their first appearance in the novel not as characters already well defined, but as indistinct presences. Properly speaking they are not individuals: their names refer to "galaxies [*nébuleuses*]" (Deleuze 2000, p. 175). Recalling what Roland Barthes suggested in a 1973 roundtable on Proust (in which, *nota bene*, Deleuze also participated),[10] we can say that the sensitivity of Proust the symptomatologist reveals a strong connection with a musical sensitivity. The idea of the character is not already available (available, even though hidden) at the beginning of the process of creation but donated only through the repetition of fragments without origin.[11] It is certainly not by chance that in *À la recherche* at a

[9] "I had the sensation of being watched by somebody who was not far off. I turned my head and saw a man of about forty, very tall and rather stout, with a very black moustache, who, nervously slapping the leg of his trousers with a switch, was staring at me, his eyes dilated with extreme attentiveness. From time to time these eyes were shot through by a look of restless activity such as the sight of a person they do not know excites only in men in whom, for whatever reason, it inspires thoughts that would not occur to anyone else—*madmen*, for instance, or spies" (Proust 1983b, p. 807, my italics).

[10] Along with Gérard Genette, Jean Ricardou and Jean-Pierre Richard. The roundtable was the final part of the colloquy "Proust et la Nouvelle Critique" organized by New York University and École normale supérieure, Paris, and held on Rue D'Ulm from 20 to 22 January 1972 (the colloquy was comprised of four conferences and two roundtables).

[11] "I would say," Barthes suggests, "that Beethoven's variations [*scil: Diabelli's variations*] function a little like Proust's work. The theme is diffracted entirely in the variations and there is no longer a varied treatment of a theme. This means that in a way the metaphor (for every idea of variation is paradigmatic) is destroyed. Or, in any case, the origin of the metaphor is destroyed. It is a metaphor, but without an origin. I think that is what should be said" (Deleuze 2007, pp. 44–45).

certain point Albertine herself—the *fille* who was born from a nebula—is the one who seems to be acknowledging and encouraging—precisely through music—in the narrator the process that we recognized as characterizing the vision of the great symptomatologist, that is to say the capacity of discovering a constellation in chaos. When Albertine "the captive" would turn into an "Angel musician" (Proust 1983e, p. 379), writes the narrator,

> she chose pieces which were either quite new or which she had played to me only once or twice, for, beginning to know me better, she was aware that I liked to fix my thoughts only upon what was still obscure to me, and to be able, in the course of these successive renderings, thanks to the increasing but, alas, distorting and alien light of my intellect, to link to one another the fragmentary and interrupted lines of the structure which at first had been almost hidden in mist. She knew and, I think, understood the joy that my mind derived, at these first hearings, from this task of modelling a still shapeless nebula (Proust 1983e, pp. 378–379).

As we should expect by now, in *À la recherche*, this process concerning the genesis of a *style* extends to all arts. In the last quotation, for example, the narrator's ears, which are imbued with what he was accustomed to hearing, struggle with music nebulas. Likewise, it is useful to recall a passage where the narrator's eyes, imbued with what he *was accustomed to seeing* struggle with an unknown literary galaxy. What is at stake, once again, is the possibility to give heed to something that forces us to recognize a new style:

> A new writer had recently begun to publish work in which the relations between things were so different from those that connected them for me that I could understand hardly anything of what he wrote. [...] Only I felt that it was not the sentence that was badly constructed but I myself that lacked the strength and agility necessary to reach the end. I would start afresh, striving tooth and nail to reach the point from which I would see the *new relationships* between things (Proust 1983c, pp. 337–338, my italics).

And in turn this can also be the case—for Proust as well as for Deleuze—in painting,[12] in theater.[13] The symptomatologist's vision is the one that catches "new relationships

[12] "There was a time at which people recognised things quite easily when it was Fromentin who had painted them, and could not recognise them at all when it was Renoir" (Proust 1983c, p. 338).

[13] See Deleuze 2000, pp. 34–38.

between things," the vision that is able to catch sight of links, at the very 'place' where no one suspected they could be: it is, as we will now see, the capability of rendering oneself sensitive to signs.

4. Healthy Literature

Thus, if we talk of Proust's 'symptomatologist vision', we do not refer exclusively to the medical field. Thanks to this power of vision, the narrator can acquire new insight into all human domains, as far as the laws of love, and his use of metaphors—either concerning medical aspects[14] or of any other kind—can be seen not so much as a means of enriching his prose but as ways of bringing to light invisible connections between domains which seemed so far apart.[15]

Now, the next step we have to take into account consists in trying to show how this particular sensitivity to symptoms corresponds to a peculiar interest in impersonal signs, in the signs of an "impersonal element":[16] precisely when literature as health—as we anticipated above—discovers the possibility to "liberate" some "life" (Deleuze 1998, p. 2). The first chapter of *Essays Critical and Clinical* significantly focuses on such a relationship between literature and *Life*. Well, it is not surprising that the book's epigraph is Proust's: "Great books are written in a kind of foreign

---

14 "She had not known, naturally, when this fatal moment would come, had never been certain, any more than those lovers whom a similar doubt leads alternately to found unreasonable hopes and unjustified suspicions on the fidelity of their mistresses" (Proust 1983c, p. 326).

15 "Truth will be attained by him [*scil:* the writer] only when he takes two different objects, states the connexion between them—a connexion analogous in the world of art to the unique connexion which in the world of science is provided by the law of causality—and encloses them in the necessary links of a well-wrought style" (Proust 1983f., pp. 924–925).

16 For example, in the case of Masoch, "the coldness of the masochistic ideal [...] is not the negation of feeling but rather the disavowal of sensuality. It is as if sentimentality assumed in this instance the superior role of the impersonal element, while sensuality held us prisoner of the particularities and imperfections of secondary nature" (Deleuze 1991, p. 52).

language (*Contre Sainte-Beuve*)." This 'being foreign' that Deleuze appeals for with Proust is strongly related not only to the notion of *outside* we recalled in the first paragraph but also to that of "becoming." And once again according to a necessary nexus: "writing," Deleuze states, "is *inseparable* from becoming." In 'healthy writing', for Deleuze, one *becomes* something else "to the point of becoming-imperceptible" (Deleuze 1998, p. 1, my italics). It seems that we are facing quite a paradox here.

Deleuze is trying to express what for him is a healthy type of literature, and, in order to do that, he is suggesting that the healthy literary work of art is the one in which the author, as it were, disappears. The becoming-imperceptible of the author can be understood in these terms.[17] What becomes imperceptible in writing is exactly what Maurice Merleau-Ponty called the "empirical man" (Merleau-Ponty 2013, p. 118), that is to say—to express it once again in Deleuzian terms—my personal story, which cannot 'cover' "the secret part of the event."[18]

At the same time, it must be specified that "to become" does not mean to renounce one's empirical part in order "to attain a form (identification, imitation, Mimesis) but to find the zone of proximity" (Deleuze 1998, p. 1). The author does not *become* by becoming 'something else', some other form that would preexist him or her. To clarify any doubts: becoming is not imitating, it is not to become something that we were supposed to adhere to before the process of becoming started. This, accor-

---

17 "The most important book about the event, more important even than those of Stendhal, Hugo, and Tolstoy, is Stephen Crane's *The Red Badge of Courage*, in which the hero designates himself anonymously as 'the young man' or 'the young soldier'" (Deleuze 1990, p. 101).

18 "What is this secret part of the event that is at once distinguished from its own realization, from its own actualization, even though realization does not exist on the outside? [...] It is what can be conveyed by all expression, or what can be realized by all realizations, the *Eventum tantum* to which the body and soul attempt to be equal, but that never stops happening and that never ceases to await us: a pure virtuality and possibility, the world in the fashion of a Stoic Incorporeal, the pure predicate" (Deleuze 1993, pp. 105–106).

ding to Deleuze, would still introduce an Aristotelian slant to the understanding of this problem.[19] Rather, Deleuze (with Félix Guattari) states clearly in *What is Philosophy?*, the artist as a "becomer" is also a "seer" (Deleuze & Guattari 1994, p. 171), and being a "seer," in the Deleuzian sense, presupposes—in a way that will appear more clear in my last paragraph—a non-empirical use of the artist's eyes. In *What is Philosophy?* "dwell[ing]" on the question of the writer, Deleuze and Guattari aim to once and for all dispel the misunderstanding regarding the relationship between our 'empirical I' and the 'becoming I':

> Many people think that novels can be created with *our* perceptions and affections, *our* memories and archives, *our* travels and fantasies, *our* children and parents, with the interesting characters we have met and, above all, the interesting character who is inevitably oneself (who isn't interesting?), and finally with our opinions holding it all together (Deleuze & Guattari 1994, p. 170, my italics).

In this case, particular attention is to be placed on the possessive pronoun *our*: "In fact, the artist, including the novelist, goes beyond the perceptual states and affective transitions of the lived" (Deleuze & Guattari 1994, p. 171). It is in this very sense, as we have just pointed out, that "the artist is a seer, a becomer" (Deleuze & Guattari 1994, p. 171). As far as writers—as artists—are concerned, Deleuze and Guattari say they work with "specific materials," that is to say "words and syntax" (Deleuze & Guattari 1994, p. 167). It is through a lifelong struggle with these materials that—if they ever manage to do it—they come to produce "a block of sensations, a pure being of sensations" (Deleuze & Guattari 1994, p. 167). An 'empirical man' experiences *his* or *her* perceptions and affections. Conversely, a 'becoming I' discovers—or we should say 'creates'—percepts and affects, namely perceptions and affections which are no more 'his'/'hers' than someone else's. In the case of Proust: the symptomato-

[19] In this regard see, for example, the way in which Deleuze reads the famous Rimbaud's formula "*Je est un autre*" in the Vincennes lecture on Kant of 21 March 1978 (the text of this lecture is available at: http://www.webdeleuze.com/php/texte.php?cle=59&groupe=Kant&langue=1).

logist becomes sensitive to symptoms that are impersonal signs. What kind of body is needed to experience such symptoms? And what kind of faculties?

Even in writing a work that could be considered as a cathedral of memory, Proust, they assert, does not work with *his* memory. What is the sense of this statement that in truth sounds quite paradoxical? All the more that they distrust not only memory "which summons forth only old perceptions" (Deleuze & Guattari 1994, p. 167), the memory of Habitus, voluntary memory (the one that according to Proust can only give us back arid snapshots of the past and that according to Deleuze would be truly analogous to the cinematographic procedure of flashback[20]), but also—and this is the most unexpected aspect, given that we are talking about Proust—involuntary memory. "Memory," they state "plays a small part in art (even and especially in Proust)" (Deleuze & Guattari 1994, p. 167).

To put this in other terms, we might suggest as follows: involuntary memory plays a major role in the famous passage in which the narrator as *apprentice*[21] tastes the well-known *madeleine*. But he has to transcend the experience of reminiscence by art, creating an eternity whose secret is no longer his own memory. An artistic block must be created. The work of art becomes, in a very paradoxical way, a "monument" (Deleuze & Guattari 1994, p. 168) which *does not* celebrate the past. The work of art as a monument does not celebrate empirical memories. The novel as a monument cannot celebrate what happened, but rather the non-empirical *event* that insists in what happens without being reduced to the empirical facts that actualized it. For that very reason, "memory, I hate you" (Deleuze & Guattari 1994, p. 168)

20 See Deleuze 1989, p. 39.

21 "The Search is oriented to the future, not to the past. Learning is essentially concerned with *signs*. Signs are the object of a temporal apprenticeship, not of an abstract knowledge" (Deleuze 2000, p. 4).

becomes the writer's formula. This is the case in Proust as well, and above all: "We attain to the percept and the affect only as to autonomous and sufficient beings that no longer owe anything to those who experience or have experienced them: Combray like it never was, is, or will be lived; Combray as cathedral or monument" (Deleuze & Guattari 1994, p. 168). The empirical material has to be brought to the point at which impersonal life can be sensed to insist in it.

5. The Fifth "World of Signs"

Finally, it is worth pointing to the fact that in 1976 Deleuze decided to add a last part of text to his *Proust and Signs*. On the grounds of what we said so far, the title of this last chapter sounds very significant: "Presence and Function of Madness: The Spider." Actually, this addition consists of a "text first published in 1973 (Deleuze 1973) and subsequently revised" (Deleuze 2000, p. ix), which in turn develops some of the principal ideas Deleuze had exposed in the 1972 roundtable on Proust that we mentioned above. Also in this case, the Deleuzian discourse makes immediately clear that it is not going to focus on an 'empirical I', that it is not going to refer to the 'empirical Marcel Proust'.

Questioning the presence of madness in *À la recherche*, Deleuze is not asking whether Proust was "mad" (Deleuze 2000, p. 170) or not. Indeed, "this question certainly has no meaning" (Deleuze 2000, p. 170). Rather, the overcoming of the 'empirical Proust' finds expression here in the concept of the "Body without organs." In fact, "the narrator" turns out to be "an enormous Body without organs" (Deleuze 2000, p. 181). Of course, it is not that the narrator does not have empirical organs. He clearly has a heart, eyes, a nose, but, for instance, in the famous "scene of the first kiss he gives Albertine, [...] he complains that we have no adequate organ to perform such an action that fills our lips, stuffs our nose, and closes our eyes" (Deleuze 2000, p. 181). On that occasion, something strange happens. He "los[es] the use of his lips, his eyes, his nose" (Deleuze 2000, p. 176).[22] Nevertheless, it is exactly "'from these hateful signs'" that he "recognizes [...] that he is in the process of kissing the beloved being" (Deleuze 2000, p. 176).

On another occasion, in *Le Temps retrouvé (Time Regained)*, the reading of the Goncourt brothers' Journal appears to reveal to him his ineptitude in hearing and seeing: "I closed the Journal of the Goncourts. [...] Certainly, I had never concealed from myself that I knew neither how to listen nor, once I was not alone, how to look. My eyes were blind to the sort of necklace an old woman might be wearing, and the things I might be told about her pearls never entered my ears" (Proust 1983f., p. 737).

Notwithstanding, the ineptitude in seeing and hearing what the Goncourt brothers were able to painstakingly describe in their Journal makes it possible for the narrator to recognize himself as a *seer,* as a *becomer.* He realizes that his ineffectiveness in seeing what the Goncourts' eyes recorded with such accuracy is not due to his blindness. Or, better, it is due to a form of selective blindness: that of a seer, so to say. This condition forces him to react to a different level of reality, normally invisible. He seems to remain numb when he faces individuals and yet to swiftly react when he encounters essences, symptoms defining ideas: "There was in me a personage who knew more or less how to look, but it was an intermittent personage, coming to life only in the presence of some general essence common to a number of things, these essences being its nourishment and its joy" (Proust 1983f., pp. 737–738). However,

22 Translation modified.

this personage cannot be voluntarily summoned by the narrator. Among the different "personages" who inhabit him, this is a whimsical one, who responds exclusively when a sign excites him giving him *pleasure*:[23] "the stories that people told escaped me, for that interested me was not what they were trying to say but the manner in which they said it and the way in which this manner revealed their characters or their *foibles*" (Proust 1983f., p. 738, my italics).

But there is more (and this last Proustian reference to *absurdity* is already a clue in this new direction). In the very last words Deleuze adds to his powerful work on Proust, it seems that he is advocating for a possibility to discover a further "world of signs" in *À la recherche*, besides those he already described in the first part (and first version) of the book.[24] Among the signs the narrator proves to be particularly reactive to, Deleuze now decisively includes the symptoms of madness. In the healthy act of writing that gives birth to Proust's masterwork (healthy insofar it frees "Life," even when that means a lot of pain for the author's empirical body), Deleuze also recognizes the *presence of Madness*, a world of symptoms expressing madness. We have just recalled that, according to Deleuze, it is not important to determine whether the 'empirical man' Marcel Proust is mad or not. But, that being said, it might still be asked: What about the narrator?

In truth, Deleuze explicitly discusses the signs of madness by referring to the two great constellations we mentioned above: Charlus and Albertine. However, the fact that he concludes his book on Proust choosing to question the narrator himself is not

---

[23] "As soon as I perceived this my intelligence [...] at once set off *joyously* in pursuit, but its quarry then, for instance the identity of the Verdurin drawing-room in various places and at various times, was situated in the middle distance, behind actual appearances, in a zone that was rather more withdrawn" (Proust 1983f., p. 738, my italics).

[24] These four worlds of signs are famously those of the "wordly signs," "love," "sensuous impressions or qualities" and "art" (see Deleuze 2000, chapter 1).

to be ignored. Reacting to these series of symptoms of Madness, the narrator—Deleuze suggests—is actually expressing his own madness. Ultimately, the last world of signs introduced and surveyed by the French philosopher would affect the *Recherche's* main character as well, that is to say, it would affect the creator of all other characters.

We have already seen how, according to Deleuze, "Proust presents the narrator as incapable of seeing, of perceiving, of remembering, of understanding..., etc." (Deleuze 2000, p. 181). This is the reason why Deleuze chooses to call him a "spider"; insofar as a "spider too sees nothing, perceives nothing, remembers nothing" (Deleuze 2000, p. 181). Correspondingly, *À la recherche* monument—a 'monument' in the sense specified in the previous paragraph—is not "constructed like a cathedral or like a gown" (Deleuze 2000, p. 182). Rather, it is built like a "web" (Deleuze 2000, p. 182). Despite its specific—empirical—blindness, the spider is no less sensitive to something that, in turn, is not less important than what it, the spider, cannot see: "it receives only the slightest vibration at the edge of its web, which propagates itself in its body as an intensive wave and sends it leaping to the necessary place" (Deleuze 2000, pp. 181–182).[25] Here we see at work the important lesson of the transcendental use of faculties Deleuze developed in *Difference and Repetition*. We could say that the "spider-Narrator, whose web is the Search being spun,"[26] has no organs which function in the empirical regime, in the voluntary regime. Nevertheless, "a faculty functions within him when constrained and obliged to do so" (Deleuze 2000, p. 182): when that happens, the "corresponding organ wakens within him," but without functioning at an empirical level that could be measured

25 Translation modified.

26 Deleuze 2000, p. 182. "This is what interests me now in the *Search*: the presence, the immanence of madness in a work that is not a dress, not a cathedral, but a spider web woven before our eyes" (Deleuze 2007, p. 33).

in the same way as "extensive quantities" (Deleuze 1994, p. 237). What is "roused" is instead an "*intensive outline*" (Deleuze 2000, p. 182). The narrator's gaze is not capable of equaling the accuracy and the variety of the Goncourt brothers', yet it is able to intensively penetrate a richer dimension that, as it where, whispers at the surface of the things. We are dealing with an intense body that undergoes intense involuntary reactions to symptoms. In this transcendental spider-body Deleuze sees "the narrator, the spy, the policeman, the jealous lover, the interpreter" and finally, also the "madman," "the universal schizophrenic who will send out a thread toward Charlus the paranoiac, another thread toward Albertine the eteromaniac, in order to make them so many *marionettes* of his own delirium, so many intensive powers of his organless body, so many profiles of *his own madness*" (Deleuze 2000, p. 182, my italics). Madness (and precisely the madness of the spider) then becomes the last word of *Proust and Signs*, the last diagnosis expressed by the Proustian "human comedy" (Deleuze 2000, p. 177).

References

Barthes, R. et al. 2007, "Proust Round Table" in: G Deleuze, *Two Regimes of Madness: Texts and Interviews 1975–1995*, Semiotext(e), New York, pp. 29–60.

Béhar, S. 1993, *L'univers médical de Proust,* La Page et la Plume, Paris.

Bizub, E. 2006, *Proust et le moi divisé. La Recherche : creuset de la psychologie expérimentale (1874–1914)*, Droz, Geneva.

Deleuze, G. 1973, "Présence et fonction de la folie dans la *Recherche du temps perdu*" *in Saggi e ricerche di letteratura francese,* vol. XII, pp. 380–390.

Deleuze, G. 1989, *Cinema 2: The Time Image,* Athlone Press, London.

Deleuze, G. 1990, *Logic of Sense,* Athlone Press, London.

Deleuze, G. 1991, *Masochism: Coldness and Cruelty & Venus in Furs,* Zone Books, New York.

Deleuze, G. 1993, *The Fold Leibniz and the Baroque,* Athlone Press, London.

Deleuze, G. 1994, *Difference and Repetition,* Columbia University Press, New York.

Deleuze, G. 1998, *Essays Critical and Clinical,* Verso, London & New York.

Deleuze, G. 2000, *Proust and Signs: The Complete Text,* University of Minnesota Press, Minneapolis.

Deleuze, G. 2004, *Desert Islands and Other Texts, 1953–1974,* Semiotext(e), New York.

Deleuze, G. 2007, *Two Regimes of Madness: Texts and Interviews 1975–1995,* Semiotext(e), New York.

Deleuze, G. & Guattari, F. 1994, *What Is Philosophy?*, Columbia University Press, New York.

Ferré, A. 1959, *Les années de collège de Marcel Proust,* Gallimard, Paris.

Fraisse, L. 2013, *L'éclectisme philosophique de Marcel Proust,* Presses de l'Université Paris-Sorbonne, Paris.

Genin, C. 1999, "La culture médicale de Marcel Proust" in: *Marcel Proust, l'écriture et les arts,* ed J-Y Tadié, Gallimard, Paris, pp. 102–109.

Merleau-Ponty, M. 2013, *Recherches sur l'usage littéraire du langage. Cours au Collège de France. Notes 1953*, MētisPresses, Geneva.

Proust, M. 1983a, *Swann's Way: Remembrance of Things Past*, vol. 1, Penguin Books, London.

Proust, M. 1983b, *Within a Budding Grove: Remembrance of Things Past,* vol. 1, Penguin Books, London.

Proust, M. 1983c, *The Guermantes Way: Remembrance of Things Past*, vol. 2, Penguin Books, London.

Proust, M. 1983d, *Cities of the Plain: Remembrance of Things Past*, vol. 2, Penguin Books, London.

Proust, M. 1983e, *The Captive: Remembrance of Things Past*, vol. 3, Penguin Books, London.

Proust, M. 1983f, *Time Regained: Remembrance of Things Past*, vol. 3, Penguin Books, London.

Tadié, J-Y. 2000, *Marcel Proust: A Life,* Viking, New York.

Painting versus Theatre: Hysteria of the Hand

3

Sjoerd van Tuinen

Mannerist Gestures

In several essays on gesture, Giorgio Agamben argues that the discovery and rise of the Gilles de la Tourette syndrome—a movement disorder which consists of ataxia, tics and dystonia—towards the end of the nineteenth century reveals "a generalized catastrophe of the sphere of gestures" (Agamben 2000, p. 51). Just as the contemporary catchall diagnosis of hysteria, from which it is distinguished yet to which it is complementary, Tourette syndrome marks a general loss of form. Everything happens as if the previously existing link between form and content, speech and act, or more generally between soul and body, is broken. People begin to stutter in language or move stiffly like automatons, interrupted by uncontrollable jerking and shuddering. The world of the bourgeoisie as a whole begins to look more and more artificial and incomplete. No longer in possession of its exterior symbols, it "succumbs to interiority and gives itself up to psychology" (Agamben 2000, p. 53).

But having lost its gestures, the bourgeoisie at the same time becomes obsessed with them. This is reflected by the rise of new forms of art. Besides the films of Étienne-Jules Marey and the Lumière brothers, Agamben points to the proto-cinematic dynamograms of Eadward Muybridge (a series of split-second photographs) and Tourette (made with a footprint method). We can also think of the theater of hysteria set up by Jean-Martin Charcot at the Hôpital de la Salpêtriere. It's not that there was no previous interest in gesture, but rather that gesture now rises to the surface in its pure mediality. No longer serving a purpose, whether that of beauty or that of communication, gesture reveals nothing but itself. It becomes a "means without end," an autonomous praxis or expressionism in which art and life intersect (Agamben 2000, p. 58).

Bringing together Aby Warburg and Gilles Deleuze, Agamben argues that a gesture that reveals itself may be understood as a *Pathosformel* or a crystal: both image and movement, it retains the tension between a phenomenal reification/obliteration and a noumenal potentiality/movement (*dynamis*) even as it stiffens historical processes into its "destiny" (Agamben 2000, pp. 53–55). Instead of a psychologically reduced notion of the image, a gesture is an "image-act," a power of visibility that gives form to affect.[1] Uniting affect and percept, it does not exist outside the image that is produced in it, but it is simultaneously the latter's genetic moment. To speak of the movement of images or the life of art, if this is to be taken literally and not just metaphorically, is to refer to this expressive unity of the image and its affective condition. When Henri Bergson denounced images of movement in space as "cinematographic illusions" based on the empirical succession of stoppages, which according to the paradox of Zeno ultimately renders all movement impossible, he therefore simultaneously argued that the real movement of images is intensive and durational. Irreducible to the representation of consciousness (the idealism of psychological qualities) or the representation of a thing (the realism of physical quantities), an image is first of all a pure *appearing:* a gestural contraction (the memory or

[1] The concept of "image-act" is developed by Horst Bredekamp's *Theorie des Bildakts. Frankfurter Vorlesungen* (2010 Suhrkamp Verlag, Berlin). Contemporary enactivists have argued that not all physical images are phenomenal images, because while the phenomenal consists of objects or things, physics consists of action. It is only because the image acts, i. e. expresses a capacity to affect and to be affected, that it can be called alive. E. g. Arteaga 2011, 'Die Lebendigkeit des Bildes. Ansätze einer enaktivischen Begründung', in: *Sehen und Handeln*, eds Horst Bredekamp and John Michael Krois, Akademie Verlag, Berlin.

manner of the image) of the immediate presence, invisible by nature, of the activity or forces of the world (the ground or matter of the image). Gesture or manner is nothing but this rising forth of the image; it is its striving or making visible as such, its *ethos* or *manerie*.[2]

Precisely to the extent that the discontinuous representation is only the destiny of gesture, even the most eternal pose in painting is never just an immobile cut, but also the fragment of a struggle or combat with other forces or possibilities. "Even the *Mona Lisa*, even *Las Meninas* could be seen not as immovable and eternal forms, but as fragments of a gesture or a still of a last film wherein only they would regain their true meaning" (Agamben 2000, pp. 55–56). But when the gesture is made in this classical manner, power and act, naturalness and style, contingency and necessity remain indiscernible in the image. All painting does, it seems, is to faithfully reproduce the empirical world that accords with our sensory-motor schema. This is also the case in the tight contractions of organic activity—perception, affection, action...—that we see in the movement-images of Hollywood cinema, which renders visible real becoming only as deriving from movement in space. Artistic imagination is reduced to the mere memory of habitual perception centered on the organic body: the cliché. For the difference of matter and manner—which Gottfried Boehm has called "iconic difference"—to appear, and for art to increase its imagination-potential and acquire mastery over it, it is necessary that this coincidence between

[2] In *The Coming Community*, Agamben discusses the scholastic concept of *manerie* as a non-classical (i. e. non-Aristotelean) principle of individuation. Instead of being either general or particular, a modal or adverbial individuation such as "grass of this manner" is both singular and universal. Like exemplars, maneries are sets or classes which are part of the totality they define. Because of this self-inclusiveness, they cannot be appropriated or predicated and rather constitute a "free use of the self". Knowing neither essence nor existence, they are the "thusness" of being, its pure "rising forth" (Agamben 2007, pp. 27–30).

time and space is upheaved.[3] This is why experiences of inoperativity—estrangement, suspension, indifference, failure, boredom, loneliness or some other crisis of purposeful action—are essential to poetic acts. As Agamben explains, the poetic act is not a habitual transition from potentiality to actuality. Rather, it feeds on resistance to creation: to have the potential of art is for the artist also to have the potential not to act (and remain an artist). Or in the words of Deleuze: "A creator's someone who creates their own impossibilities, and thereby creates possibilities." [4] Art implies a pathogenesis which turns an image or a form into the symptom of invisible forces whose present becomings exceed it. From the wrought pose in theatre to deformation in figurative painting to transgressive framing in architecture (to the nonsense word in philosophy), it puts forward new, decentered body images that act on the virtual and reveal possible worlds where existing possibilities are exhausted.

Of old, art history has identified such moments of breakdown and breakthrough in art as mannerist. Agamben, too, argues that real mastery shows itself in imperfection, or in an "inner mannerism". It is this inner mannerism that defines the style

[3] Iconic difference is the contrast between the material basis of images and the events of their appearance. Preceding semantics, the iconic event differentiates the actual representing and the representational function of the image. While this event cannot exist outside material things, it does not coincide with their properties and therefore remains ideal. It is a pure possibility, i. e. the capacity of images to become visible. With Deleuze we can also define this event with the Peircean concept of firstness, which concerns only what is new in experience. It is a pure becoming, a fresh, fleeting and nevertheless eternal affect: "It is not a sensation, a feeling, an idea, but the quality of a possible sensation, feeling or idea. Firstness is thus the category of the Possible: it gives a proper consistency to the possible, it expresses the possible without actualizing it, whilst making it a complete mode" (Deleuze 1986, p. 98). In what follows, I use iconic difference as a mannerist concept, since it emphasizes the manner or modality rather than the aspect or quality in which something differs. Instead of asking *what* images are, the pertinent question is *how* they become.

[4] Deleuze illustrates his point with the "Egyptian postures" of tennis player John McEnroe: "As with McEnroe, it's by banging your head on the wall that you find a way through. You have to work on the wall, because without a set of impossibilities, you won't have the line of flight, the exit that is creation, the power of falsity that is truth" (Deleuze 1995, p. 133).

of an artist, even when this style only crystallizes as such late in life or at the end of an epoch.[5] Mannerism is the art of composition that emphasizes its own composedness. It makes language speak the fact that it is speaking, just as it makes painting paint the fact of painting. Full of repetition, artificiality and suspense, it reveals an element of expression in which nothing is represented and nothing completed. Seen in this element, the precision and perfection in the endless permutations of random gestures and impossible poses in the work of Samuel Beckett is just as mannerist as the unfinished sculptures of Michelangelo, the deformations of Parmigianino, the contrived postures of Rosso, the psychotic ecstacy in El Greco, the enigmatic *concetti* in Tesauro or the polished dissonances in Gesualdo. In each case, we discover an art that produces and exhibits its own medial enduring in its spontaneous, irreversible and absolute self-determination. Mannerism is thus the art of immanence as artistic potentiality: based entirely on autonomous, self-referential or auto-objective expressions, it is the diligent art of a pure and perpetual gestuality that is also the art of a "relentless Spinozism"[6] (Deleuze 1998, p. 152; Deleuze & Guattari 1987, p. 317).

---

5 Agamben equates mannerism with lateness, discovering a mannerism in the late Plato, the late Shakespeare, the late Titian (*Tiziano fecit fecit*, made and unmade it) and so on. In each case, we find a poetics of inoperativity, an undoing in the doing or acting without making something. See Agamben, G 2014 ,Resistance in Art', European Graduate School Lecture Series (video file). Available at <https://www.youtube.com/watch?t=25&v=WQTljKtkrJQ> [15 July 2015, inactive].

6 In *Expressionism in Philosophy: Spinoza,* Deleuze shows how modal individuation does not presuppose any subjective mediation, but proceeds as immediate expression of an infinite depth (implied substance) at the surface (explication). Bodies and souls are thus defined by the transpassibility or pathos through which they relate to their genetic principle. All analogy between them is due to their principle of production, which effectively turns the body into a mechanism just it turns the soul into a spiritual automaton exposed to exterior forces.

The El Greco Fallacy

Ever since the word was first coined, the rise of mannerism has been explained in pathogenic terms. In psychiatry, manneredness signifies a change of expressional behavior in mimicry, inadequate choice of words, pathetic emphasis on tones in speech, or awkward gestures. Its symptomatology emerged at around the same time that the concept of mannerism made its appearance in art history.[7] Even if we accept that mannerism is the symptom of a crisis of classicism as the sign of a sensory-motor collapse, however, a crisis never suffices to explain the destiny images find in art. Such a reduction would make us guilty of a version of what has come to be known as the "El Greco fallacy," namely to posit that deformed figures in El Greco's art reflect an underlying perceptual elongation of objects caused by the painter's supposed astigmatism, whereas in fact, the composition of line and color on the canvas produces a genuinely new, inhuman gesture-image. While the crisis of the bourgeoisie as a specific mode of living coincides with the invention of cinema, similarly, the invention of the cinematic gesture implies the invention of a new possibility or visibility, a "third eye," which is not simply the eye of the camera that registers what happens

[7] In Vienna of the 1920's, "everybody spoke of mannerism" (Gombrich & Eribon, cited in Kris, Falguieres & Gombrich 2005, p. 197). After Wilhelm Pinder's "physiognomics of mannerism" (1932), the main inspiration for later discussions is Ludwig Binswanger's famous Heideggerian theses on manneredness (Binswanger 1956, pp. 324–418): "Als wesentlich für die Manieriertheit … erwies sich uns das angsterfüllte, verzweifelte Nicht-Selbstseinkönnen, ineins mit der Haltsuche an einem Vor-Bild aus der Öffentlichkeit des Man und der Überbetonung dieses Vor-Bildes zur *Verdeckung* der Heimatlosigkeit, Weltunsicherheit und Bedrohtheit der Existenz" (Binswanger 1956, p. 239).

before the human eye, but the eye of montage.[8] It may be that art always emerges from the experience of something too large in life, as Deleuze frequently puts it, but its creativity is found only in the manner in which it rises to its material occasion and renders its conditions visible in a "bloc of sensations" that is also a "monument" of its own future. While the Renaissance, just as cubism four centuries later, decomposes and recomposes a spatial movement that is already taken for granted, mannerism thus raises a question common to all the arts, namely how to give form to its own becoming: "How will sensation be able to sufficiently turn in on itself, relax or contract itself, so as to capture these nongiven forces in what it gives us, to make us sense these insensible forces, and raise itself to its own conditions? It is in this way that music must render nonsonorous forces sonorous, and painting must render invisible forces visible" (Deleuze 2003, pp. 56–57).

Mannerism, to the extent that it is a movement of permanent renewal through gestures that are irreducible to some external cause or a general system of meaning and codification, is an ongoing de- and recodification of classicism. No longer communicating an already given content or continuing an already given form or discipline, it turns words into pre-linguistic cries just as figures become pre-pictorial poses and refrains pre-musical expressions. Agamben argues that with mannerism, art acquires a general "mutism" which is that of mime theatre. (Agamben 2000, pp. 59–60) Because the theatre does not exist outside the gestures that produce it, Deleuze speaks

8 "This is not a human eye—even an improved one. For, although the human eye can surmount some of its limitations with the help of contraptions and instruments, there is one which it cannot surmount, since it is its own condition of possibility. Its relative immobility as a receptive organ means that all images vary for a single one, in relation to a privileged image. And, if the camera is considered as apparatus for shooting film, it is subject to the same conditioning limitation. But the cinema is not simply the camera: it is montage. And if from the point of view of the human eye, montage is undoubtedly a construction, from the point of view of another eye, it ceases to be one; it is the pure vision of a non-human eye, of an eye which would be in things" (Deleuze 1986, p. 81).

of a theatre of repetition rather than of representation.[9] But why impose on this immediate self-exhibition of pure corporal mediality the conditions of theatre, even if they are supposedly stretched beyond their limits towards an Artaudian theatre of cruelty where the distance between representation and presence approaches zero? The reason there are multiple arts is precisely that each art produces its own irreducible manner of putting itself forward, based on its own clinical definition of and solution to the critical or vital problem from which it arises. To reduce mannerism to theatre, by contrast, is to reduce gesture to a general psychological strategy of representing a reality that is already lost just as art is reduced to the symbol of a passage from life to death. In *The Ideology of the Traitor. Art, Manner and Mannerism* (originally published 1976), for example, the famous Italian art critic Achille Bonito Oliva depicts mannerism as a "betrayal of life", which expresses itself in the highly intellectualized body "language" of a negative dialectic. Art would lose its immediate "frontal" grip on the "desiring machines" of political and economical reality and compensate for its imperfection with the "lateral", melancholic and self-deceiving psychology of the alienated, disinterested and guilty individual artist who seeks perfection in the "false" spectacle of the models and ceremonial gestures of the court. The essence of mannerism, in other words, would be the aporia of art's self-distancing from "the simple dramatic urgency of life" into a world of mere "simulacra" founded on the "denial of its own impossibility" (Oliva 1998, especially pp. 59–71, 128). Clearly this isolated world of metaphorical and metonymical representations is quite the

[9] "In the theatre of repetition, we experience pure forces, dynamic lines in space which act without intermediary upon the spirit, and link it directly with nature and history, with a language which speaks before words, with gestures which develop before organized bodies, with masks before faces, with spectres and phantoms before characters" (Deleuze 2001, p. 10).

opposite of the gestural breakthrough we started out with, as it is entirely founded on a pathological escapism which itself doesn't need art to come about.

In order to understand the living reality of mannerism, we must therefore return the masks from the paralyzed representation of some lost content to the material expression of an exterior potential that is at the same time at the heart of them. Following Félix Guattari, this implies that we no longer hold on to any institutional definition of art and replace it with a clinical onto-aesthetics of asignifying signs in constant flux and interaction. Art is not imaginary, but makes things function differently, assembling lines of flight where existing possibilities are depleted. It is not some vulgarized version of the Freudian sublimation of suffering into "virtual reality." If it can nonetheless be called hysterical or even schizophrenic, then because it gives the hysterics or schizophrenics a visible or audible consistency or "body" which they do not yet possess and which is everywhere repressed or reduced in the established institutions ("Someone asked us if we had ever seen a schizophrenic—no, no, we have never seen one" (Deleuze & Guattari 2003, p. 380)). As Deleuze argues, it is music itself that is schizophrenic, just as hysteria is the "clinical essence" of the mode of existence of painting. Schizophrenia and hysteria are not generic lifestyles (the former doesn't even present itself as such), just as music or painting are not generic domains. Rather, they are singularizing modalities of life itself.

Painting: Hysteria and Hysteresis

Elsewhere I have already explored in detail Deleuze's discussion of hysteria as the ethico-aesthetical mode in which painting constantly reinvents itself in response to its vital "problematics": the face-landscape schematism that constitutes the persistent intensive production of the prepictorial surface of visibility as such.[10] It is by creating its own, relatively immobile body of line and color that painting can become elastic enough to capture and render visible the aberrant movements or animal becomings that are insistent in this abstract machine of "facialization" of classical representation. If the surface of the canvas is always already virtually filtered and classified into a system of figurative probabilities and clichés by black lines on a white surface, painting introduces line strokes and color-patches that give the surface a new relief and reveal the line as a matrix for colors to come.[11] Thus by contracting the face-landscape system into its own practice, painting becomes capable of immanently infecting this system with counter-rhythmical manual traits that lead to unexpected consequences, first of all the liberation of the eye from its functional adherence to the organism.[12] This is why, instead of departing from the digital division of labour in which the hand executes the discrete visions of the eye, Deleuze throughout *The Logic of Sensation* follows the analog traces of the gestures that shake up the hand's

---

[10] Van Tuinen, S, 'Mannerism and Hysteria: On the Mode of Existence of Painting' forthcoming in *What Images Do*, eds. J. Bäcklund, H. Oxvig & M. Søberg, Aarhus University Press, Aarhus.

[11] Deleuze & Guattari 1987, p. 173. The German word for painting, *Malerei*, derives from the Latin *macula*, mark, stain, blotch or spot, while the Italian word for sketch is *schizzo*. Cf. Giorgio Vasari: "We call sketches a first type of drawing, used to find the postures and initial composition of the work; and they are made in the form of a splotch, ... a rough sketch that just serves as a first try. And because of the draughtman's fury they are quickly executed with quill or other instrument or charcoal only to try the soul of what they remember, which is why we call them sketches" (Vasari 1991, 1: 156).

[12] As Jakub Zdebik (2012, pp. 97–108) has pointed out, the French word *trait* used by Deleuze means both facial feature and stroke of a pencil or a brush.

dependence in the production of the image at the same time that they irritate optical space and give the eye itself a haptic quality.[13] The figure remains a recognizable visual reality, but is now inseparable from a "catastrophe" that dissolves the optical logic into the formless space of a restless movement.

In the end, there is no painting without a whole depth of field that both destabilizes it and authorizes its existence, but it is in mannerism that this depth rises to surface as such.[14] This explains the extreme prominence given to the hand (*la mano*) in mannerist painting. The relative anestheticization of the eye and the paralyzation of the motor body go together with a strange contracture and hyperestheticization of the hand. The neurasthenic hand is the privileged hysterogenic zone of painting and the privileged power of visibility, that is, the privileged organ for expressing all sort of "unnatural" or "nonorganic" mannerisms. From Michelangelo and Bronzino to Parmigianino to Tintoretto, mannerist painting is the hysteria or excessive presence of the hand in all its obtrusiveness.

Characteristic of mannerism, then, is less a dissociated attitude towards the world, which is only its psychologization, than a "dissociation of the senses," as T. S. Eliot described the metaphysical poetry of John Donne, namely a dissociation which im-

---

13 "The two definitions of painting, by line and color, and by the trait and the color-patch, do not overlap exactly, for the first is visual but the second is manual. To describe the relationship of the eye and the hand, and the values through which this relation passes, it is obviously not enough to say that the eye judges and the hands execute. The relationship between the hand and the eye is infinitely rich, passing through dynamic tensions, logical reversals, and organic exchanges and substitutions" (Deleuze 2004, p. 154).

14 Following Heinrich Wölfflin, Deleuze argues that there is a depth of field "when an element of a plane refers directly to an element of a different plane, when characters address each other directly from one plane to another, in an organization of the picture along the diagonal [Tintoretto], or through a gap which thus priviliges the background and brings it into immediate touch with the foreground [Rubens]. The picture is 'internally hollowed out' [Wölfflin]. At this moment, depth becomes depth *of* field, whilst the dimensions of the foreground take on an abnormal size, and those of the background are reduced, in a violent perspective which does even more to unite the near and the faraway" (Deleuze 1989, pp. 107–108).

mediately also implies a "distortion of sense" (Deleuze 2001, pp. 305–306). This is also the essence of what Antonin Artaud calls a "body without organs": a body that is not so much opposed to organs as to their organization in the organism. To construct a body without organs, Deleuze and Guattari write, is to "walk on your head, sing with your sinuses, see through your skin, breathe with your belly", as in the body lanced by arrows of Tintoretto's *St. Sebastian* (1579–81) (Deleuze & Guattari 1987, pp. 151, 178). For the ancient Greeks, hysteria meant the wandering of the uterus across the body. In mannerist painting, the same happens to the eye, which, under constant pressure of the hand, becomes a power of visibility that migrates through the body. Thus hysteria is ecstatic yet it remains a corporeal experience, dependent on a redistribution of what acts and what sees on an aesthetical plane of composition that is not before the image (evidence) nor behind the image (representation), but its very milieu. In art, the body discovers itself not as a model, but as potential visibility, a hysterical power of the false that can be raised to the *n*th power from the moment it is made to communicate with "unnatural" becomings.

Bacon shares this invention of this particular temporality of the painted figure with his mannerist predecessors, in particular Michelangelo and his followers. "To put time inside the Figure—this is the force of bodies in Bacon: the large male back as variation" (Deleuze 2004, p. 48). It is true that painting spatializes matter by arresting it in a *station hystérique*, an interruption of vital movement. But it does so not in order to cut out a stable form but to register and reveal the event or manner of an irreversible metamorphosis that escapes the present.[15] Thus if painting maintains a hysterical relation to the abstract machine of facialization, then it is to the extent that it restores the face (its general given content) to the more abstract life of the body (its singular expression) and takes visibility to a higher power beyond the organic qualification of face and landscape. In Michelangelo, it produces a passage from the face to the head, with eyes wide-open and full of terror, and then also from the head to the body, "a mass of sheer physical being that seems to move like some highly powered automaton" (Bellosi 1970, p. 21). Here, hysteria no longer belongs to the painted model or to the painter himself, who had already abandoned himself in a reckless and "almost hysterical" way to the canvas (Deleuze 2004, pp. 96, 98), but becomes a purely pictorial (f)act, irreducible to the ordinary life world. Before hysteria constitutes a general symptomatology, it is a singular and real gesture.[16]

According to Deleuze, the key invention of mannerist painting was "the Figure in its pure state," (Deleuze 2004, p. 161) in other words, a non-figurative use of visual figuration that exposes clichéd forms of representation to the immediate and excessive presence of sensation. The figural, Deleuze writes, is a "zone of objective indiscernibility or indeterminability" (Deleuze 2004, pp. 157, 21), in which stable forms give way to interminable deformation. The fact of movement is not a transformation from one form to another, but a movement immanent to form itself, similar to the retardation of the effect when the causal forces acting upon a body are

---

15 Thus there is no contradiction between saying that "[w]hat fascinates Bacon is not movement, but its effect on an immobile body" (Deleuze 2004, p. xi) and that "the oeuvre of Francis Bacon is entirely dedicated to movement" (Leclerq 2002, p. 8). More generally we can say that to capture metamorphosis is to invent the instant that captures the no longer and the not yet ("hysteresis"). Representation is only the degree-zero of such a capture.

16 "Of all the arts, painting is undoubtedly the only one that necessarily, 'hysterically,' integrates its own catastrophe, and consequently is constituted as a flight in advance. In the other arts, the catastrophe is only associated. But painters pass through the catastrophe themselves, embrace the chaos, and attempt to emerge from it" (Deleuze 2004, pp. 102–103).

changed: "Bacon's whole 'style' takes place in a beforehand and an afterward: what takes place before the painting has even begun, but also what takes place afterward, a hysteresis that will break off the work each time, interrupt its figurative course, and yet give it back afterward…" (Deleuze 2004, p. 50). In physics, hysteresis means the dependence of a system not only on its current environment but also on its past environment. This dependence arises because the system can be in more than one internal state, such that relations between cause and effect, past and future are non-linear (plasticity) and sometimes even reversible (elasticity).[17] But whereas physics (or history) tends to translate coexisting, metastable becomings into a succession (Deleuze & Guattari 1987, p. 430), art seeks precisely their potentialization. Hysteria or hysteresis is arguably what Georges Didi-Huberman has called the *Nachleben* of the image and what Jean-Francois Lyotard calls the *lapsus* that distinguishes the figure from figuration.[18] In El Greco or Tintoretto, Deleuze discovers a hysteresis that "gives definition to the formal powers of the raw material, which rise to the surface and are put forward as so many detours or folds," each of which is itself a new "condition of variation" (Deleuze 1993, p. 17–18). As the recursive process in which new, unforeseen folds can be extracted from an existing form, hysteresis is the physical expression for the reciprocal determination of forces in the becoming of the work of art. While these folds make for a spectacular visual content, they are also the physical expression of the very forces at work as so many of its "feminine,

[17] This hysterical effect as emergence within a field of potential also appears in philosophy, for example when Sartre in the *Critique of Dialectical Reason* speaks of hysteresis as the principle by which the development of history lags behind, is pitted against itself, intricately regresses within its progressions, thus making impossible any historical totality. See Gibson 2001, pp. 19–20.

[18] Didi-Huberman 2010, pp. 301–302. Didi-Huberman opposes *Nachleben* as a "counter-rhythm," an artificial contraction, to vital movement. (Ibid., p. 212) Lyotard 2011, p. 129.

animal, molecular detours" (Deleuze 1989, p. 2). Comparable perhaps to Russian formalism, where form reveals itself as the sum of its deformations, mannerist painting relies on what Bacon, with respect to Henri Michaux's self-described "cinematic" drawings and painting from his mescaline period, describes as "delayed ways of remaking the human figure" (Sylvester 1987, pp. 61–63). There is an intricate tension between movement and paralysis, as if the form of expression still refers back to a stable form of content, while the form of content has already partly dissolved into the form of expression where it attains an hallucinatory otherness or excessive presence. Looking at a mannerist figure, it is as if we are looking into a crystal ball that reveals to us all sorts of possible worlds at the same time, vaguely distinct but held together by a broken line or an indefinite color field.

The Clinical Superiority of Painting over Theater

In order to understand the critical and clinical value of this understanding of painting as hysteresis guided by the hand, and more generally the relation between suffering and art, let us return to the concept of hysteria in psychology. Deleuze's concept of hysteria is closer to Charcot than to Freud (Geyskens 2008, pp. 301–302). Whereas Freud reduced physical and affective madness to symbolic representations or symptoms of psychological memories or fantasies, Charcot interpreted hysteria as a physiological process. Or paraphrasing Didi-Huberman: as Charcot was watching, Freud listened. In fact, Charcot was as much a visual artist as a clinical therapist. Not only did he turn the Salpetrière hospital into a scene for the spectacle of hysteria, including masked balls for doctors and patients, he also created hundreds of sketches and photos of hysterics in his painter's workshop. Charcot's photography thus mediated between the fantasy of hysteria and the fantasy of knowledge: "A reciprocity of charm was instituted between physicians, with their insatiable desire for images of Hysteria, and hysterics, who willingly participated and actually raised the stakes through their increasingly theatricalized bodies" (Didi-Huberman 2004, p. xi).

Yet in the case of the star doctors and the star hysterics, as Didi-Huberman emphasizes, we are still dealing with fantasies. By reinventing the event of hysteria as physical spectacle and sensational representation, Charcot can't seem to decide between knowledge and art, psychology and physiology. Does the opulent visibility of the pain of a body in the throes of its symptoms really give us insight in the forces that effectively cause this pain, let alone enable us to deflect them in one way or another? Aren't both the doctor and the patient too much stuck in representation for critically and clinically diagnosing the actual presence of hysteria? And isn't this precisely the reason why Bacon repeatedly emphasizes, in conversation with David Sylvester, that painting is about expressing the event of "the scream more than the horror" (Deleuze 2004, p. 38).

Perhaps Charcot's problem is that he is not able to distinguish between the eye of the camera and the eye of painting. It is a problem similar to that of Muybridge's attempts to photograph the movement of a horse. While the latter wanted to avoid the effect of stagedness by cutting up movement in a series of equidistant poses, he nonetheless produced only an illusion of movement in extension (which Bergson calls the "cinematographic illusion" (Bergson 1998, pp. 306–307)) all the while letting the intensity of real movement, that of the horse as well as of the space through which the horse moves, escape. Taking himself more for a scientist than for an artist, Muybridge was not interested in the singular and open-ended synthesis of real movement that takes place invisibly between the poses. Instead, he sought to extract movement as a general quality of instants in a universal space and time. He thus analytically reduced a complex of qualitatively different durations to the single duration of the time of mechanics in which movement can only appear as already made. Similarly, Charcot used the objective eye of the camera to record the clichéd staging of the primal scene of hysteria, centralizing his subjects as if the photographic image were a transparently legible entity and the body expressed itself in an equally transparent manner. But in this way, the representation of hysteria completely evaporates the experience of excessive presence from which it emerged in the first place.

What Charcot and Muybridge reveal is that science typically moves from condition to result, or from reality to fiction. Art, by contrast, typically passes from fiction to reality. Or as Didi-Huberman puts it: whereas Charcot sought to determine the symptom, Warburg needed its overdetermination or openness (Didi-Huberman 2010, pp. 319–325). To express movement is not to concord with reality (photography), but on the contrary to expose the possible in order to make real. As Marie-José Mondzain has argued, a painted image is a situation, not a photograph. It has its specific economy of compossibilities and incompossibilities by which it struggles with the invisible and by which the invisible becomes present in the image (Mondzain 2005).[19] The further painting is from "reality"—and thus the more potential movement it expresses—the more it elliptically enjoins it. (Leclerq 2002, p. 52) The more artificial his portrait of Michel Leiris becomes, Bacon explains, the more it resembles him (Sylvester 1987, p. 146). If theatre and photography merely expose the effectuation of movement in the body they represent, could painting rise up to

[19] Or as Jean-Luc Nancy puts it, the image is never "of" the thing, rather, in the translation into visibility something of the thing is always lost: "[t]he image disputes the presence of the thing" (Nancy 2005, p. 21).

the condition of visibility of the body? While Charcot molds the body according to the abstract symptomatology of hysteria and Muybridge subordinates it to an equally abstract image of animality, isn't Bacon after something much more concrete, namely to capture the living (animal) manners of hysteria and sports themselves?

To answer these questions positively is to claim the right to determine what hysteria is, i. e. to produce its reason, for art rather than for science. Even in those cases where psychoanalysis may be factually true, it does not automatically possess the right to define hysteria as such, as this presupposes that the fact is taken together with its genetic condition, i. e. the real construction of hysteria as the autonomous bloc of sensation.[20] Thus while theater and photography provide general conditions of judging over an established fact, conditions which are not hysterical at all, painting renders visible an aberrant movement that remains invisible and unreal on the stage of psychoanalysis. Rather than representing the world, the economical—or rather, ecological—problem of painting is how to compose dissimilar strata of matter and life into a visible world.[21] While every image of reality is constructed through the aggregate movement of its material elements, this movement is not realized by these elements but authorizes their actual existence and remains unlocalizable or "metaphysical" itself. The clinical superiority of painting over theater lies in its capacity to

[20] As David Lapoujade has recently argued, facts in themselves matter little from the perspective of a transcendental empiricism in which the conditions have to be created together with the fact. Rather, every fact has to be understood as a pretention, a demand or a claim. By what right can Oedipus be affirmed as universal? Certainly not on the grounds of "general" family life. Following Nietzsche, only the extreme and singular cases—"aberrant movements"—count. The question of the well-foundedness of a claim (*quid juris?*) is inseparable from the expressivity of the claim as such (Lapoujade 2014, p. 18). It therefore does not mean "Is this true hysteria?" but "Whose vision is it?"—the scientist-physician or the artist-physician? (Cf. Didi-Hubermann 2010, p. 117).

[21] Joselit 2014, pp. 92–103, esp. 94. Joselit argues that in art, "[r]ather than representing something stable by closely warranting images to a substrate, the objective here is to invent new formats for generating configurations of images" (Joselit 2014, p. 98).

literally render visible this excessive presence of movement or action as a constantly changing configuration in the metaphorical image of hysteria.[22] Only painting is adequate to hysteria, since it takes us from the effect of hysteria to its cause. It does so by rendering the heterogeneity of causes and the singularity of their effect indiscernible in the figure. It doesn't merely invoke or evoke hysteria, which would be a redundant, tautological, and intransitive quality isolated as sensible quality and comparable to hysterical behaviour in general, but produces an intensive quantity, the unity of a movement in the act of being made.[23] In mannerist painting, then, the body discovers itself not as a theatrical model, but as body without qualities: the body as power of visibility, a power of the false that can be raised to the *n*th power if, by means of hystericization, it is made to communicate with external forces in a nonorganic becoming. As Hauser says, "[a] mannerist work is not an image of reality, but rather a conglomerate of contributions to its image" (Hauser 1979, p. 25). By making its own duration correspond with the movement at hand, by reconstituting and recomposing the conditions and dispositions of movement, painting critically interprets the facts of mental illness (the who, where, and when of hysteria), but at the same time clinically evaluates their becoming and necessity (what/how is hysteria?). Like the other arts, mannerist painting is a combat with its own shadow, but

[22] Presence in painting should be conceived in analogy to what Deleuze—again following Artaud's contrast of the psychological and optical theatre of passion based on its agonizing distance to reality and danger and the physical and synaesthetic theatre of cruelty which allows no gap between life and theatre (Artaud 1993, p. 84)—calls the "excess of theatricality … that only cinema can give to theatre" (Deleuze 1989, p. 84). Hysteria is precisely the excess of theatricality that painting gives to theatre through its own physical means.

[23] Prévost, forthcoming 2015.

hysteria is the visible modality in which this combat takes place in painting.[24] Only in painting is hysteria no longer a model but a necessity for the artistic production of its proper consistency, that is, of hysteria in its pure state.

Of course, Bacon too let himself be inspired by the photos taken during Charcot's performances in the Salpètrière as well as the photo series of Muybridge, which register the movements of hysterical humans and animals per fraction of a second, such that a turned nose can resemble the trunk of a pig and a grin the beak of a dog. Yet these optical resemblances are only the effects of an instantaneous becoming or sympathy that belongs neither to animals nor to humans, but that forms an autonomous bloc of sensation. Similarity in products should not be compared to similarity in their production. Only the painter, Deleuze argues, can render visible this non-localizable relation that hysterics have with the groans and grunts of animals, a relation which is not based on identification or empathy, nor on sadism, but based on a "pity" with life as suffering (Deleuze 2003, pp. 23–26). If this pity is expressed in the scream as pathic becoming instead of a psychic representation of horror, this is because in the scream the separation between human and animal, art and nature, disappears. The scream is an autonomous expression and if it scares us, this is because of its gesture and not vice versa.[25] Bacon's hysterical screams are not pathological states of the soul, but gestures or lived abstractions: moments of crisis and spiritual passage from the spasm to the smile: "This is not a hysteria of the painter, but a hysteria of pain-

24 "When, like a wrestler, the visible body confronts the powers of the invisible, it gives them no other visibility than its own. It is within this visibility that the body actively struggles, affirming the possibility of triumphing, which was beyond reach as long as these powers remained invisible, hidden in a spectacle that sapped our strength and diverted us" (Deleuze 2003, p. 62).

25 Since perception and action coincide in the gesture, as William James famously argued, we are afraid of the bear because we run from it and not vice versa. (James 1884)

ting. ... What the hysteric is incapable of doing—a little art—is accomplished in painting. [...] Painting transmutes this cerebral pessimism into nervous optimism. Painting is hysteria, or converts hysteria, because it makes presence immediately visible" (Deleuze 2003, p. 52). Psychological hysteria and physical hysteresis meet in the sense that many hysteric systems, for example electromagnetic systems such as a microphone connected to a tape-recorder, make screeching noises as they respond to changes in their external load. Such is also Bacon's self-declared realism: to paint "what happens", i. e. to render visible the actual life of visual images. A vitalist expressionism replaces psychological expressionism. To the question why the pope screams, Deleuze replies: because he sees nothing (Deleuze 2003, p. 61). The pope screams, but his voice is silenced by the surrounding curtains while his face and view are fragmented by the dark, warm colors. They register the forces that invest the figure and deform it into a spastic percept without the appearance of a new image that reinstalls psychological content. Hysteria is now a real, physical sensation that precedes all interiority. No longer a lived state of the organically personalized body, it is a pictorial act, a creative process. A mannerism *hors l'asile.*

But if everything revolves around the presence of invisible forces instead of their representation, then why does Bacon need any figurative violence or any representation of this relation between painting and hysteria at all? We might ask the same question of some mannerist painters, or more still, of psychoanalytical interpretations of mannerism. In fact, the later Bacon, painting more and more in the *grande maniera* of the old masters, repeatedly distanced himself from the overtly sensational character of his early works. With the hysterical smiles of Bacon's 1953 *Portrait and Human Head*, or the 1955 *Pope*, the spectacle of violence still appears as an aim in itself. It is not yet the grimace as pure intensity, in which nothing is to be seen and in which nonetheless everything happens: a painful feeling in the mouth that instantaneously releases a laughter in which the mouth no longer serves to communicate but functions as the hole through which the organic body disappears. Bacon became more and more interested in the immobile movements that fill up and singularize the figure from within, especially in the case of Velazquez sitting figures, and that cannot be represented by any external quality or gesture developed in space. In the end, as he himself explained, he had always tried to paint a smile in a similar way as Monet painted a sunset or Lewis Carroll imagined the grin without the cat (Sylvester 1987, p. 50); that is, as purely impersonal powers of expression and expressions of a purely impersonal capacity of living. For whenever existing forms of living are exhausted, art incorporates new forms of life, and the more modest and restrained these forms are, the more indistinguishable the multiplicity of movement becomes, the more powerful they impose themselves. "Sobriety sobriety" (Deleuze & Guattari 1987, p. 344): there is no better way of turning readymade effects into potentializing affects and reintegrating what appears to be merely mannered with a new manner. This is the great Deleuzian paradox of a "mannerism of sobriety" (Deleuze & Guattari 1986, p. 79): "In the end, the maximum violence will be found in the seated or crouching Figures, which are subjected to neither torture nor brutality, to which nothing visible happens, and yet which manifest the power of the paint all the more" (Deleuze 2003, pp. 38–39).

The BwO of Mannerist Painting

It is of course true that, with mannerism, there also appears a kind of parapsychology based on the dissociation between posture and situation, the former having become unconditioned with all action suspended. Bronzino and Parmigianino disturb the classical harmony between body and mind, the motor and the sensory. They have put forward a frozen type of figure, detached spirits that assume affected poses without in the least seeming to feel them, since an artful formality obscures or conceals their nature. Their extreme ceremoniality—with their armor or corsets as rigid masks—gives them only an artificial posture within an untenable situation. Likewise, Pontormo worked in extreme isolation, thus enforcing a deep scission between the bio-social life and the pedantry of art. In the strange, sideways glance of mannerist figures, there is no momentariness at all: the Figure is not caught in any act (Oliva 1998, pp. 159–160). In fact, the crystalline perfection of mannerist images puts into everything the proximity of death. But contrary to a psychology based on theater and photography, should we not rather say that painting judges death from the point of view of life or the will to art instead of vice versa, such that the painter succeeds in tracing a line of flight precisely where the hysteric fails?

Once more, it's a matter of changing our perspective from content to gesture. According to Aloïs Riegl, art originates in an inorganic, crystalline motif which enables it to express nature in its own manner, i. e. to compete with nature rather than imitating it (Riegl 2004, pp. 123–124). Much later, Hauser would speak more specifically of "the 'inorganic' structure of mannerist works" (Hauser 1979, p. 24), i. e. their materially heterogenetic nature. For both, the apparently sterile figures are not just fantasies, significances or subjectifications, but also real experimentations and constructed machinations of sensation. In a word: they are not lost souls, but cracked bodies, body-images or bodies of sensation (Deleuze & Guattari 1987, p. 150; Deleuze 2003, p. 47). Drawing on Castiglione's treatment of the aristocratic virtue of sophisticated *disinvoltura*, what has often been characterized as the disembodied and elitist levity and sophistication of the "stylish style" (Shearman 1977, p. 19) turns out to be not just a disinterested and frivolous demonstration of technique or a forced escape into manneredness, but the outcome of a veritable creation of new, artificial assemblages of life where existing possibilities and organic surfaces have been exhausted. This exhaustion is not a psychological state, but an exhaustion of all psychology. Even the aristocratic quality of mannerist art is perhaps less that of the courtier than that of an anonymous grandeur.[26] It is indeed as if the figures have fallen back from life and are reabsorbed in the crystal (cf. Deleuze 1989, pp. 87–88). But contrary to a sublimation of life in mannered indifference, style becomes the very condition of life in a Nietzschean sense: a life that belongs to no one and that cannot be sustained organically, but that finds its singular consistency in a Great Style and a Great Health capable of raising "lived perceptions to the percept and lived affections to the affect" (Deleuze & Guattari 1994, pp. 170–171).

Deleuze reinterprets this living discrepancy between soul and body as the intensive fact of the body which can only be sensed at the limit of the human, lived body. If "'[m]annerism' is one of the most pathetic traits of schizophrenia" (Deleuze 1993, p. 152 n. 23; Deleuze 1989, p. 230; Deleuze & Guattari 1985, p. 548 n. 16), this is because the mannerist artist is like the "schizo-artisan" whose hallucinations are "as close as possible to matter, to a burning, living centre of matter" (Deleuze & Guattari

[26] 'Because affect is not a personal feeling… it is the effectuation of a power of the pack that throws the self into upheaval and makes it real.' (Deleuze & Guattari, 1987, p. 240)

2003, pp. 19, 87) and who is struggling to preserve life in itself even in the face of his organic disintegration.[27] This new mode of living should not be conceived of in continuity with the organic body, as its prosthetic extension, but rather as a fissure or a crack through which the organism "escapes from itself" with the "affective athleticism"—another reference to Artaud—of an immobile convulsion (Deleuze 2003, pp. 18, 40; Deleuze & Guattari 1994, p. 162). In Bacon, this crack appears as the mouth, the anus, the throat, the toilet, the mirror or the washbasin through which the hysterical figures escape from themselves in a spastic act of loving, vomiting or excrementing. In Parmigianino or Bronzino, it is the elongated fingers by which the figure dissipates into a strange floating architecture following the transversal line of, for example, a folded table cloth.[28] We are dealing with specific bodies without organs, singular manners of sensation that integrate the visibility of the organic body with its material outside. Art is not a regression, but a creation of manners of being traversed by new intensities.

[27] Deleuze and Guattari define hysteria by the territorializing function, whereas depression/paranoia is related to despotic overcoding and schizophrenia to capitalist decoding of desire (Deleuze & Guattari 2003, p. 33).

[28] In *Hochrenaissance, Manierismus, Frühbarock,* Hans Hoffmann speaks of the *Raumflucht* that is typical of mannerist images.

References

Agamben, G. 2000, *Means without End: Notes on Politics,* trans. V. Binetti and C. Casarino, University of Minnesota Press, Minneapolis/London.

Agamben, G. 2005, *State of Exception,* trans. K. Attell, University of Chicago Press, London.

Artaud, A. 1993, *The Theatre and its Double,* trans. V. Corti, Calder Publications, London.

Arteaga, A. 2011, 'Die Lebendigkeit des Bildes. Ansätze einer enaktivischen Begründung', in: *Sehen und Handeln*, eds.: Horst Bredekamp and John Michael Krois, Akademie Verlag, Berlin, pp. 45–63.

Bergson, H. 1998, *Creative Evolution,* trans. A. Mitchell, Dover Publications, New York.

Binswanger, L. 1956, *Drei Formen missglückten Daseins: Verstiegenheit, Verschrobenheit,* Manieriertheit, De Gruyter, Berlin.

Deleuze, G. & Guattari, F 1986, *Kafka. Toward a Minor Literature,* trans. D. Polan, University of Minnesota Press, Minneapolis.

Deleuze, G. & Guattari, F 1994, *What is Philosophy?*, trans. H. Tomlinson and G. Burchill, Verso, London/New York.

Deleuze, G. & Guattari, F 2003, *Anti-Oedipus. Capitalism and Schizophrenia,* trans. R. Hurley, M. Seem, and H. R. Lane, Continuum, London/New York.

Deleuze, G. 1989, *Cinema 2: The Time Image,* trans. H. Tomlinson and R. Galeta, University of Minnesota Press, Minneapolis.

Deleuze, G. 1993, *The Fold. Leibniz and the Baroque,* trans. T. Conley, University of Minnesota Press, Minneapolis.

Deleuze, G. 1995, *Negotiations. 1972–1990*, trans. Martin Joughin, Columbia University Press, New York.

Deleuze, G. 1998, *Essays Critical and Clinical,* trans. D. W. Smith and M. A. Greco, Verso, London/New York.

Deleuze, G. 2001, *Difference and Repetition,* trans. P. Patton, Continuum, New York/London.

Deleuze, G. 2003, *Kant's Critical Philosophy,* trans. H. Tomlinson and B. Habberjam, University of Minnesota Press, Minneapolis.

Deleuze, G. 2004, *Francis Bacon. The Logic of Sensation,* trans. D. W. Smith, Continuum, London/New York.

Deleuze, G. & Guattari, F 1987, *A Thousand Plateaus. Capitalism and Schizophrenia,* trans. B. Massumi, University of Minnesota Press, Minneapolis.

Deleuze, G. 1986, *Cinema 1: The Movement-Image,* trans. H. Tomlinson and B. Habberjam, University of Minnesota Press, Minneapolis.

Didi-Huberman, G. 2004, *Invention of Hysteria: Charcot and the Photographic Iconography of the Salpêtrière,* trans. A. Hartz, MIT Press, Cambridge/London.

Didi-Huberman, G. 2010, *Das Nachleben der Bilder. Kunstgeschichte und Phantomzeit nach Aby Warburg,* trans. M. Bischoff, Suhrkamp Verlag, Berlin, pp. 301–302.

Geyskens, T. 2008, 'Gilles Deleuze over Francis Bacon. Schilderkunst als hysterie', in:Tijdschrift voor Filosofie, 70/2008, pp. 297–316.

Gibson, A. 2011, *Intermittency. The Concept of Historical Reason in Recent French Philosophy* Edinburgh University Press, Edinburgh, pp. 19–20.

Hauser, A. 1979, *Der Ursprung der modernen Kunst und Literatur: Die Entwicklung des Manierismus seit der Krise der Renaissance,* C H Beck, München, p. 15.

James, W. 1884, *What is an emotion?* Available from: <http://psychclassics.yorku.ca/James/emotion.htm> [12 October 2015].

Joselit, D. 2014, 'Against Representation', *Texte zur Kunst,* vol. 24, no. 95.

Kris, E., Falquières, P. and Gombrich, E. 2005. *Le Style rustique. Le moulage d'après nature chez Wenzel Jamnitzer et Bernard Palissy,* Macula, Paris.

Lapoujade, D. 2014, *Deleuze, Les Mouvements Aberrants,* Les Éditions de Minuit, Paris.

Luciano B. 1970, *Michelangelo: Painting,* trans. G. Webb, Thames and Hudson, London, p. 21.

Lyotard, J. F. 2011, *Discourse, Figure,* trans. A. Hudek and M. Lydon, University of Minnesota Press, Minneapolis, p. 129.

Nancy, J. 2005, *The Ground of the Image,* trans. J. Fort, University Press, Fordham.

Oliva, A. B. 1998, *The Ideology of the Traitor: Art, Manner and Mannerism,* trans. M. Eaton & P. Metcalfe, Electa, Milan.

Prévost, B. forthcoming 2015, 'Puissance de l'art, force des images, intensités esthétiques' in *Speculative Art Histories,* ed Sjoerd van Tuinen, Mimesis International, Milan/London.

Riegl, A. 2004, *Historical Grammar of the Visual Arts,* trans. J. E. Jung, MIT Press, Berkely.

Shearman, J. 1977, *Mannerism. Style and Civilization,* Penguin, London.

Sylvester, D. 1987, *The Brutality of Fact: Interviews with Francis Bacon,* Thames & Hudson, New York.

Vasari, G. 1991, *The Lives of the Artists,* trans. J. C. Bonadella and P. Bonadella, Oxford University Press, Oxford.

Zdebik, J. 2012, *Deleuze and the Diagram: Aesthetic Threads in Visual Organization* Continuum, London, p. 97–108.

On the Figuration of Drives, or Duchamp as an Outsider

4

Stefan Kristensen

> *Il n'y a pas de solution de continuité entre la machine-célibataire et la Mariée. Mais les liens seront électriques et exprimeront ainsi la mise à nu: opération alternative. Court-circuit au besoin*
> (Duchamp 1973, p. 75).

Entire libraries have been written on the work of Marcel Duchamp, on the structure of his work, on his place in the art world and in art history, etc. This paper is an attempt to read the Duchampian oeuvre in order to characterize its relation to art works made by artists with a pathological background. The issue in so doing is to show how the drives, i. e. the movements of desire, can come to be represented and thus also presented in exhibitions. In order to do so I will present the exhibition *Bachelor Machines* conceived and curated by Harald Szeemann in 1975, featuring Duchamp among many other artists, including figures from the Prinzhorn collection in Heidelberg.[1] The question would then be: how did Szeemann justify the rapprochement? What was its actual meaning? A quick look at Duchamp's oeuvre shows that he was very interested in contemporary (non-Euclidian) geometries, and in other issues from contemporary science and epistemology, as well as in the most theoretical questions relating to chess; he professed a very cerebral and intellectual approach to art and things in general.[2] Moreover, the broadest admitted definition of outsider art is related to the subjectivity of the author: outsider art is understood as a production made by people unconscious of, or uninterested in, their status as

1 The catalogue was published by Jean Clair and Harald Szeemann in Venice the same year. It contains a great number of important texts by Szeemann himself, Michel Carrouges, Michel de Certeau, Jean-François Lyotard, Arturo Schwarz and Peter Gorsen among others.

2 Alliez (2013) explains Duchamp's relation to contemporary mathematical theory in detail (213ss).

artists.[3] From this perspective, it seems quite counter-intuitive to build a link between Duchamp and outsider art; the only way to make such a link plausible is to look at the matter represented *in* their artworks. It is well known that Szeemann's curatorial conception and practice was characterized by the idea of a "museum of obsessions," and obsessions are typically movements in the psychic sphere in relation to which the subject is passive; the subject is essentially driven by his/her obsessions.

In this study, I will present a reading of Duchamp's work along the line of a museum of obsessions focusing thereby on the visualization of desire and on the movement of projection; I will then show that Duchamp's work does present affinities with outsider art inasmuch as productions by 'outsiders' are supposed to reflect the movements of their inner drives; finally, I propose a conception of subjectivity as caught in a field of tensions, or a dialectics of subjection and drive toward emancipation, and claim that the importance of Duchamp's work is closely linked to its ability to unveil this paradoxical structure of subjectivity.

Duchamp's Machines

Marcel Duchamp is widely recognized as the key figure in the emergence of contemporary art. This status is attributed to two main works, a series of 'ready-mades', and the invention of a large number of wordplays and puns, but also, and perhaps foremost on the way he lead his life itself.[4] My concern here is to discuss his two main works from an existential perspective: They can both be considered as parts of

---

3 This is in substance the very influential conception formulated by Dubuffet in his attempt to wrest psychopathological art from the hands of the psychiatrists and to form the notion of "art brut." This is manifest in the texts written by Dubuffet in the context of the first shows he organized in the late 1940s and early 1950s; see Dubuffet 1967, pp. 175–177, pp. 198–202 and pp. 205–224.

4 For a political and aesthetical interpretation of Duchamp's life, cf. Lazzarato 2014.

the same endeavor, as the second deepens the questions opened up by the first. The first work bears two titles: *The Large Glass or The Bride Stripped Bare by Her Bachelors, Even (Le Grand Verre or La Mariée mise à nu par ses célibataires, même).* Duchamp worked on it for about eight years, between 1915 and 1923, shortly after having abandoned his painting practice. After a long interruption, where he played with the idea of becoming a professional chess player (see Marcadé 2007, pp. 241–245), he started to work in secret on another big project after the end of the Second World War: this became the installation *Etant donnés: 1° la chute d'eau, 2° le gaz d'éclairage (Given: 1. the Waterfall, 2. the Illuminating Gas)*, which he finished in 1966, two years before his death. In the following passages I will successively propose a close reading of these two works, claiming that they must be understood as being what Deleuze and Guattari call "desiring machines," in other words that they present a peculiar figuration of the way our desires are produced. This is no new interpretation; the critic Jean Clair noted already in 1975 that, "one of the richest and most recent interpretations of the *Large Glass* remains the one of Deleuze and Guattari in the first pages of the *Anti-Oedipus*" (Clair 1975, p. 22). In following this suggestion by Clair, we can show not only that Duchamp proposed a fecund strategy of the figuration of subjectivity understood as a desiring being, but also of subjectivity understood as a singular balance between activity and passivity. This, I would like to claim, is implied in Deleuze and Guattari's concept of the machine which draws precisely on, among other sources, Duchamp's "bachelor machine." The figuration of a desiring subjectivity is not anthropomorphic; it is situated on the plane of desire itself, but since it poses a question of perspective, of what a point of view is, it bears an essential feature of human subjectivity. As Sebastian Egenhofer noted more recently,

> [P]erspective is not a secondary topic in Duchamp. The reflection on perspective—spatial-geometrical perspective concentrating the image of the world on a here, and temporal perspective centering the image on a now moving with the consciousness of the subject—structures his whole work.[5] (Egenhofer 2010, p. 79)

In summation, my claim is that Duchamp's machines show the articulation of desire and perception, or more precisely, the fundamental desiring nature of perception, and that this subordination of perception under the movements of desire is what Deleuze and Guattari call a "desiring machine." Only in this way it is possible to conceive of the link between Duchamp and outsider art. In other terms, he makes visible the invisible structures of desire, but in a highly conscious way, whereas the authors of outsider art are mostly unreflective about their creations.[6] A careful reader has perhaps already here noticed my rather interchangeable use of the terms "drive" and "desire". This is due their respective ambiguity, but also to the way Deleuze and Guattari (my main philosophical reference here) use the terms, as equivalent. In *Anti-Oedipus*, one of the main sources of the notion of "desiring machine" is Leopold Szondi's theory of drives because he understands the drives primarily as non symbolic forces that the subject has to integrate into his / her existential realm. The only aspect they criticize in Szondi's approach is that he projects the drives onto a range of predefined categories, thereby restricting the contingency and singularity of their expression. Deleuze and Guattari introduce the notion of "desiring machine", or more simply "desire," in order to account for the production of unexpected contents.[7]

5 On this same topic, see Clair's 1977 essay "Thaumaturgus opticus" (Clair 2000, p. 63–110).

6 At least according to the commonplace opinion on the matter since Dubuffet; see above, note 3.

7 See Deleuze and Guattari 1983, pp. 289–290.

The Large Glass and the Figuration of Drives

How is all this supposed to work? At first glance, one would think that the representation of the unconscious as productive space in constant movement is quite alien to the functions of *Large Glass*. It doesn't seem to produce anything, its appearance is rather static. The question is, firstly, the articulation of the movement of desire and the projection of the gaze, of perspective. Duchamp himself wrote very explicitly about the question of perspective in notes that have been found in the "Green Box," I will be focusing in this passage mainly on geometrical and theoretical issues, and leaving questions about subjective experience aside.[8] In his conversations with Pierre Cabanne, he states that "perspective was very important. The *Large Glass* constitutes a rehabilitation of perspective that had been completely ignored, denigrated. Perspective, with me, became absolutely scientific." (Duchamp 2014, p. 39) In the following passages, I will refer both implicitly and explicitly to a number of classical and recent commentaries on Duchamp, while leaving all the esoteric or religious interpretations aside as well as those interpretations attempting to place Duchamp in the history of Western art.[9] My question here, as already mentioned, concerns the conjunction, or the articulation, of visual perception and the movement of desire. Since the two great works can be considered as two versions, or perspectives, of the same idea I will make a close analysis of the *Large Glass* and then see how *Etant donnés* complements the construction of the former. My main argument is that any gaze, any projection has an affective component, a movement toward its object, and that this is precisely the movement that Duchamp sought to represent.

---

[8] Cf. Duchamp 1973, p. 86–90. The texts of the *Green Box* were established and published by Michel Sanouillet in *Duchamp du signe* (Duchamp 1973).

[9] Octavio Paz (1990), Jean Clair (1975, 2000), Lyotard (1977), but also more recently Jones (1995), Egenhofer (2010), Lageira (2013), Alliez (2013) and Lazzarato (2014).

The *Large Glass* is a glass panel divided in two equal parts, one above the other; the lower part is the space of the bachelors whereas the upper part is the one of the bride. I will spare a precise description of the work because it is very famous and also because there are already beautiful descriptions to be found in the critical literature.[10] The work is completed by a sort of user manual consisting in a series of notes kept in the *Green Box* published as a box in 1934, more than ten years after Duchamp "definitively abandoned" the work. Thus, the splitting of the work is not only visual, into an upper and a lower part, but also between the visual and the discursive through the ten-year gap between the end of Duchamp's work on the *Glass* and the publishing of the texts, since the *Green Box* can be considered a part of the work itself. The first feature of the *Large Glass* is precisely the tension aroused by this splitting, both spatial and temporal. The bachelor machines in the lower part are separated from the bride by the gap between the two parts of the glass, but their movement is entirely directed towards the bride with no means to reach her, a spatial tension accentuated by the undertitle of the work: *Delay in glass (Retard en verre).*[11] The fact that Duchamp himself called his work a "delay" and not a "picture" is of course a way of embedding a temporal dimension into the work; and the temporal delay, or gap, was deliberately arranged by Duchamp since the texts of the *Green Box* were all written in 1914. In the visual structure of the *Large Glass*, the tension is made up by the interactions between the bride and the machinery of the bachelors. As the title suggests *(The Bride stripped bare by its Bachelors...)*, there is a movement of desire from the bachelors towards the top, towards the bride; they are an "architectonic

10 One of the best descriptions is in Octavio Paz (1990, p. 42ss).

11 "Use 'delay' instead of picture or painting; picture on glass becomes delay in glass—but delay in glass does not mean picture on glass" (Duchamp 1973, p. 26).

base" for the bride, and their machinery gives rise to a movement towards the bride that Duchamp calls the "desire motor" (Duchamp 1973, p. 39). There is an offer from the bachelors in the direction of the bride, and this offer is slowed down by the distance between the protagonists due to the separation of the two glasses. Duchamp writes that the bride "warmly rejects" the "bachelors' brusque offer," which makes the connections between them "electrical." The desiring movement is thus doubled and reciprocal: the "tormented gearing" of the bachelors takes the form of a motor rushing towards the bride to strip her bare, whereas the bride uses the energy transmitted to her in order to come closer to the "cinematic blossoming" which at the same time makes up "the most important part of the painting (graphically as a surface)." A fuel-like substance transmits energy from the bottom towards the top and is called "automobiline," or "love gasoline" (*essence d'amour*). Duchamp describes this "blossoming" as a process going on beneath his eyes, and not merely symbolically. The picture, he writes, "will be an inventory of the elements of this blossoming, elements of the sexual life imagined by her, the bride-desiring" (Duchamp 1973, p. 42). The movement of this visual inventory is unleashed by the text of the *Green Box*. There is a reciprocity and an interpenetration of the protagonists, so that the movements of the bachelors feed the desire of the bride, and the bride "accepts this stripping by the bachelors since she supplies the love gasoline to the sparks of this electrical stripping" (Duchamp 1973, p. 44). The whole text about the bride in the *Green Box* describes in fact a sexual act about which one cannot say whether it arrives to a conclusion or not. The term "blossoming," referring to the veil extending on the right side of the bride in upper right part of the glass, and the term "splash" (*éclaboussure*), referring to the lower right area, suggest that the act is concluded by some sort of enjoyment or pleasure. However, the structural difference between the lower area of the bachelors, dominated by strict geometrical forms and the upper area of the bride, characterized by a more indeterminate geometry, suggests an uncertainty in this respect.[12] Alliez develops a Lacanian interpretation of this uncertainty:

> The object of the *Large Glass* is not to deal metaphorically with eroticism, but rather to use its most manifest sexual load in order to feed an apparently machinic logic in the fourth dimension of a signifying (pata-)physics of discourse in unchained metamorphoses of all ambivalences. (Alliez 2013, 243 (my translation))[13]

In other terms, according to this approach, the *Large Glass* is not a metaphor of eroticism, but a language machine playing on all dimensions of ambiguity. This is certainly a legitimate interpretation, but as Duchamp himself would argue, his works are open to any interpretation as long as the explanation seems to make sense.[14] But one can also understand this ambiguity of the *Large Glass* as a means of setting the art work at the right level of generality: it is not merely an erotic image, but it is nevertheless a figuration of the movements of desire. By setting up different ambiguities in the image, Duchamp keeps his work in a relative indeterminacy which is also a sort of generality, the only generality that art can afford.

Duchamp's *Large Glass* is indeed an example of a "desiring machine" in the sense introduced by Deleuze and Guattari, inasmuch as they define the desiring machine as a complex form characterized by an anthropomorphisation of the mechanism and

---

12 See Paz 1990, p. 45ss. Paz however highlights the fact that it is not an orgasm, but an ongoing sexual intercourse. Concerning the word "blossoming," Paz notes that "Duchamp uses the word in a figurative sense: the bride blossoms, opens up, dilates with pleasure. It is not orgasm but the sensations that precede it. *The Green Box* is explicit: the blossoming "is the last state of the nude bride before the orgasm that might make her fall" (p. 43).

13 The rather complicated syntax of this quote requires that I also bring the original French: "L'objet du *Grand Verre* n'est pas de traiter métaphoriquement de l'érotisme mais plutôt d'utiliser sa charge sexuelle la plus manifeste pour alimenter une logique d'apparence machinique dans la quatrième dimension d'une (pata-)physique signifiante du discours en métamorphoses déchaînées de toutes les équivoques."

14 Marcadé quotes Arman telling that Duchamp was very "accommodating", pp. 474–475.

correlatively a mechanization of the living movements.[15] He does so by consistently using a mechanistic vocabulary and conceives the *Large Glass* as machinery in motion. But the other important aspect is the question of seeing: how does this machinery become visible? Whose desire is supposed to be represented? In other terms: how, under which perspective, does the desiring machine appear to us?

The Projection of the Gaze

As Jean Clair explains, Duchamp spent long hours studying treatise on perspective from the Renaissance during his employment at the Sainte Geneviève Library in Paris in the period between 1913 and 1915, while preparing ideas for the *Large Glass*.[16] The texts he wrote during this period were to become the content of the *Green Box*, to be published alongside the work as a user manual.[17] At the same time, his reflections about perspective developed with experiences brought about by modern techniques, particularly in relation to the landscape, with distances and speed. As commentators have remarked, his automobile trip from Paris to the Jura mountains together with Guillaume Apollinaire, Francis Picabia and the latter's wife Gabrielle Buffet in 1912 seems to have been a major source of inspiration for the piece.[18] For Duchamp, perspective is not simply a question of point of view, it is also a question

---

15 Cf. Alliez 2013, p. 168. See also Deleuze and Guattari's characterization in *Anti-Œdipus*, "Desiring-machines are both technical and social" (Deleuze & Guattari 1983, p. 32).

16 Cf. Clair 2000, pp. 63–100.

17 In the conversations with Pierre Cabanne, Duchamp explains that the *Glass* should not go without the explanations contained in the *Box* because the Glass should give rise to an experience of conjunction of the visual and the conceptual: "You had to refer to the book and see them together. The conjunction of the two removes the retinal aspect that I don't like" (Duchamp 2014, p. 45).

18 The trip is mentioned in the first texts of the *Green Box* (pp. 26–27); see also Jean Clair, "Métaphores automobiles" (Clair 2000, pp. 169–175).

of movement and even speed. One of his lesser known readymades can be mentioned in order to show the unity of speed and desire in his creation, *False Vagina*, consisting of a red Parisian number plate with the number "4936 TT 75".[19] The automobile, the color red, and the feminine body as object of desire are here concentrated in an impressive condensation. Through its machinic representation in the *Large Glass*, the feminine figure is the object of the desire of the male bachelors, the target of their movement, and at the same time, as being herself in movement, she is the figuration of this very desire. Duchamp's bride is thus like Penelope, another bride surrounded by aggressive bachelors, in the center of a tension constituting the very temporal vibration of the work.

In a similar sense, turning to Duchamp's other *magnum opus, Etant Donnés*, I'd like to highlight that its apparent immobility also expresses a vibration characterizing the movement as such.[20] The woman appears as an embodiment of the bride from the *Large Glass*. Looking through the holes in the door the spectator sees her body lying at the center of the image in the landscape, in a posture of abandon but completely immaculate, seeming to rest indefinitely on the wooden branches. Despite the separation between the spectator and the landscape secured by the door acting as a screen and the pierced brick wall behind the door the vibratory tension is nevertheless palpable. The tension is also present through the incoherencies in the image visible through the hole in the brick wall. On the one hand, the posture of the woman suggests that she might be dead, since the body's color is very pale and the scene is reminiscent of a rape scene; but on the other, this impression is at odds with the absence of any trace of violence, of red paint or any other depictions of wounds on

---

19 Cf. the catalogue *Etant Donnés* (Duchamp 2009, p. 349).

20 The best description, with images, is found in the 2009 Philadelphia catalogue (Duchamp 2009).

the body. Moreover, the enclosed and so to speak virginal aspect of the woman's sex also contradicts the impression that any violence has occurred, which confirms the description already formulated in the *Green Box* that the bride is an "apotheosis of virginity" (Duchamp 1973, p. 39). Finally, the relaxed posture of the woman's body, who is seemingly asleep, is in stark contrast to the firmness with which her hand is holding the gaslight, a tonus incompatible with the state of sleep. This contradiction is further reinforced by the impression that it must be difficult to sleep on a bunch of branches evoking the brittle quality of firewood or kindling rather than that of a straw bed.[21] All these contradictions add to the tension of the spectator's body confronted with the closed door, who must find viewing holes to look through and thus become a voyeur of this strange scene. In this sense, *Etant Donnés* is structured like a threshold where the closed door without hinges plays a crucial role. Thanks to the door, the access to the work is essentially ocular, as Jacinto Lageira remarks (Lageira 2013, p. 57–59). The door plays the role of a frame but due to its shape and to the holes in it, the act of vision requires an effort of the whole body in order to find the viewing holes and the right body posture in order to observe the scene inside from the right angle. Through the necessity of such an effort, the eyes of the spectator, and thus also the concrete corporeal perspective on the work, are placed at the center of the installation. The work is "ocular" inasmuch as the eye implicates the whole body in a sort of sensory-motor tension through which it upholds a certain posture and anticipates movement, but it is not "retinal" according to the term by which Duchamp criticized modern painting.[22] But this movement of the body doesn't happen inside

---

21 The comparison with the firewood is introduced by Octavio Paz in order to compare the bride to a convicted person on a stake.

22 See his conversations with Pierre Cabanne: "Since Courbet, we believe that painting is directed at the retina; this was everybody's mistake. [...] Before that, painting had other functions; it could be religious, philosophical, moral" (p. 45).

the installation; it remains at the threshold, and the consequence of this is that the experience of the work encompasses not only the image as seen through the door and the wall, but also, and perhaps more significantly, the very imminence of this movement that pushes at but does not go beyond the threshold creates a suspended time within which the spectator/voyeur feels movement without any displacement of their own body. This phenomenologically inspired analysis seems to me more convincing than an analysis based on a formalist and language centered approach, such as Eric Alliez's. Duchamp indeed doesn't argue against experience; he argues against the idea that visual art should address the eye only, whereas it also has the potential to mobilize (to set in motion) other aspects of our intentionality, such as tactility, conceptuality, and of course linguistic expression.

Such an interpretation of *Etant Donnés* is reinforced and confirmed by a few other elements: first the image shown in the installation is a motif arousing a movement of desire; it is ostensibly erotic, and is reminiscent of the famous Courbet painting *The Origin of the World* that Duchamp might have seen during a visit in Lacan's country house in September 1958.[23] The character lying on the branches is a nude woman, literally stripped bare and prepared for the invasive and voyeuristic gaze of the spectators. As most commentators have remarked, the closed door in this case plays the same role as the horizontal separation between the two parts of the *Large Glass*, a separation that Duchamp calls the "clothes of the bride."[24] If she is "stripped bare" in the *Large Glass*, it is because this clothing (which is also at the same time a threshold and a separation) is somehow crossed by the bachelors, but this doesn't mean that their desire is consummated. The separation between the two

23 As Bernard Marcadé supposes (Marcadé, pp. 442–443).

24 See Duchamp 1973, the schema on pp. 20–21.

spaces is clearly marked in the two works; it makes sure that there is no effective communication between them, between the bride and the bachelors in the *Large Glass*, and between the lying woman (an embodiment of the bride) and the spectator-voyeurs in *Etant Donnés*. The separation makes sure that there is no intersubjective common space between, on the one hand, an object of desire, "stripped bare", thereby suggesting that she is always already raped by the gaze of the others, and, on the other, the urge of those who remain bachelors because they embody the origin of desire, and because the desire is nourished by its chronic dissatisfaction. Second, the identification of perspective with movement is justified by the use of a duo of unexpected concepts found in the writings of the *White Box*: The polar concepts of appearance and apparition (*apparence—apparition*).[25] A quick reading of the two pages written by Duchamp on the relation between these two notions could make one think of a neo-platonic conception. On the one hand, we would have the appearance of the object in the sense of its perceptual aspect, and on the other what Duchamp calls the mold, referring the "luminous source of the object" (Duchamp 1973, p. 85). However, Duchamp explains that the appearance of the object refers to its being three dimensional, i. e. what is perceptible through the senses, whereas the apparition is two dimensional:

> This mold is not itself an object, it is the image in n-1 dimensions of the essential points of this object of n dimensions. The 3-dim'l appearance comes from the 2-dim'l apparition which is the mold of it (external form) (Duchamp 1973, p. 85).

The relation of appearance and apparition is essentially a movement, or a passage, from n-1 dimensional existence to n-dimensional existence; there is no idea in Duchamp of a more real essence of the thing "behind" its appearance, a "reality" inaccessible to

[25] These texts were published by Duchamp under the title *A l'infinitif* in 1966. Here, I'm quoting from Duchamp 1973, pp. 74–101.

the senses but accessible only to thought. There are different sensorial appearances of an object, all originating in a mold containing the appearances as virtual possibilities. Thus, the *Large Glass* can be understood as a mold, in two dimensions, of the three dimensional image of *Etant donnés*. In both cases, the position of the spectator is crucial; whereas there is no point of view internal to the artwork, the gaze of the spectator is clearly signified, both through the structure of *Etant donnés* (the doors and its holes for the spectator's eyes) and through the very movement of unfolding the gaze from the two-dimensional to the three-dimensional work. In other terms, the circuit of the gaze internal to the work, between the bride and her bachelors, is characterized by an absence of point of view—one can even speak of a blind movement inside the image. But this movement is precisely what the machine makes visible for the spectator; perspective, here, becomes a technique to make the desire figured within the work visible to the outside, to enable the spectators to embrace it with their gaze. In this way, the question of perspective pertains to visual access to the movement of desire, whereas the figuration of desire itself is independent of a conscious perspectivist position-taking. Such an analysis of the making visible of desire might remind one of Merleau-Ponty's critique of the subjective camera in his essay on *Cinema and the New Psychology*:

> We will get a much better sense of dizziness if we see it from the outside, if we contemplate that unbalanced body contorted on a rock or that unsteady step trying to adapt itself to who knows what upheaval of space. For the movies as for modern psychology dizziness, pleasure, grief, love, and hate are ways of behaving (Merleau-Ponty 1964, p. 58).

Duchamp, unlike the cinematographer, doesn't show the behavior itself, but rather the formal structure of a behavior; the vibration which is the condition for the possibility of a desiring behavior. I now turn to the task of making evident the link with outsider art.

Production and Celibacy

As I wrote in the introduction to this text, the link between Duchamp's work and outsider art is far from evident. However, by 1975 there was already a long history of linking the avant-garde movements of the early twentieth century (in particular Dada and surrealism) with art works by children and the insane.[26] Szeemann is an heir of this ancient link of Surrealism and Dadaism with psychopathological art; his interest in the sources of human creativity lead him to establish a link between art produced in psychopathological contexts and artistic strategies such as those found with Duchamp's laying bare the structures of desire, and of the movement towards the other. Szeemann was the first to rediscover the Prinzhorn collection, by conceiving and organizing an exhibition with a selection of works from the collection in 1963 at the Kunsthalle in Bern. This exhibition had a great influence and contributed widely to the integration of outsider art into large scale mainstream art events.[27] Szeemann's strategy is thus in sharp contrast to the attitude of Dubuffet who wanted to keep art of this kind away from the wider art world as such. Here I am following Szeemann's path because the conjunction of psychopathological productions and the highly intellectual constructions of Duchamp is justified in his case by a certain conception of the exhibition of art, namely the role of exhibiting the creative process. In other terms, as in Szeemann's conception, art is always also a way of showing the movement of production.

[26] A good, quite early example is the exhibition organized in 1936 by Alfred H. Barr Jr at the Museum of Modern Art in New York under the title *Fantastic Art, Dad, Surrealism*, where Duchamp presents eleven works, and which also features a few works by "insane" people as "comparative material". This "material" includes one work from the Prinzhorn collection, anonymous in the catalogue, in fact due to August Klett (case 36, table IX), one of Prinzhorn's ten "schizophrenic masters".

[27] In the *Documenta* directed by Szeemann in 1972, he also had a section devoted to Prinzhorn under the title "Bildnerei der Geisteskranken".

The very notion of the "bachelor, or celibate, machine" was formulated by the writer Michel Carrouges in a book published in 1954; he took the expression from Duchamp and used it to describe various other machines, mainly from literature (Kafka, Jarry, Roussel among others). He also played a key role in the exhibition organized by Szeemann in 1975 in which his introduction to the catalogue sets the stage. His definition of the celibate machine in the catalogue is a "fantastic image transforming love into a mechanics of death." Moreover, it is an "impossible, useless, incomprehensible, delirious" machine, i. e. a "simulacrum", "governed only by the mental laws of subjectivity" but at the same time "grounded on a mathematical logics" (Szeemann and Clair 1975, p. 21). Carrouges is also quoted in *Anti-Œdipus* as having used the Duchampian expression as a general concept designating different machines in literature; but Deleuze & Guattari ask a question that Carrouges doesn't formulate: "What does the celibate machine produce? What is produced by means of it?" (1983, p. 18). Their answer is that the celibate machine produces pure intensities; pure intensities are, they claim, particularly accessible to schizophrenic experience: "There is a schizophrenic experience of intensive quantities in their pure state, to a point that is almost unbearable," and the subjectivity who is having such experiences is the specific subject of the schizophrenic delusion, the "I" of the "I feel that I am becoming a woman" (Deleuze & Guattari 1983, p. 18) (in the case of Schreber for example). The whole passage from *Anti-Œdipus* is quoted by Szeemann in the catalogue; it was certainly a major source of inspiration and theoretical legitimation for Szeemann's strategy (pp. 19–20). Indeed, Szeemann's interest for Prinzhorn and psychopathological art on the one hand and for Duchamp's celibate machine on the other is justified by the question of the origins of creativity, by the question of production. As he writes in an introduction to the famous exhibition *When Attitudes Become Form* in 1969, "The meaning of this art lies in the fact that a whole generation of artists sets out to let the 'nature of art and artists' become 'form' in a natural process" (Szeemann 1981, p. 47). In the first text presenting the idea of a "museum of obsessions," in 1974, Szeemann situates his project as an attempt to oppose the institutionalization of art and to reset the accent onto the emotional; a museum of obsessions, he writes quoting the psychiatrist Theodor Spoerri, favors "a thinking that shows magic-animistic features, without any sharp separation between imagination and reality."[28] In this project, the celibate machines are under the category of the "obsessions of closed circuits" (Szeemann 1981, p. 105). In another programmatic text from the same period, Szeemann defines the obsession as a "primal unit of energy," completely independently of its social value or use, one which is very near the Deleuzian-Guattarian conception.[29] And in fact, Szeemann credits Deleuze and Guattari for having renewed the discourse about the notion of obsession, after the psychoanalytic tradition had seemingly evaded it. The idea that creativity is independent of its impact and reception, or even use in society is also a key aspect that links the work of Duchamp with art from insane persons. To make it brief, Szeemann's interest in Duchamp's machine is in the making visible of a closed circuit of intensities captured in glass or objects.

---

[28] Szeemann 1981, p. 103; Quoting Spoerri's *Kompendium der Psychiatrie* (Basel, 1962). Spoerri was responsible for the section devoted to psychopathological art in documenta 5.

[29] *Ibid.*, 125–126. "Obsession is a joyfully recognized, although pre-Freudian unit of energy that cannot give a damn whether it is expressed or used by society in negative, positive, harmful or beneficial ways." The text is entitled "Museum der Obsessionen", was written and first published in Geneva in 1975 at Skira, Art actuel. An English version is published in the *Catalogue of all Exhibitions*, 370–379.

To designate the machine as "celibate" thus means that it is linked to nothing other than itself and in this way it offers a figuration of the psychic energy as such, and thus a reflection on the act of creation itself. The celibate machine is not a device; it is itself a term and does not show any input or output. As mentioned above, it produces *intensities* and no objects, nothing identifiable and usable. It is the locus of an unresolved tension and constitutes therefore the pure affirmation of a perspective, of a vibratory movement tending toward an undetermined object, a movement whose vibration is a figuration of the pure possible. Duchamp expresses this very idea in a note from 1913, under the title "Possible":

> The figuration of a possible.
> (not as the opposite of impossible
> nor as related to probable
> nor as subordinated to likely)
>
> the possible is only
> a physical "caustic" [vitriol type]
> burning up all aesthetics or callistics (Duchamp 1973, p. 73)

Here Duchamp points to what is at stake in the *Large Glass*, the necessary relation between an image of the pure possible and the absence of the aesthetic dimension. Of course the expression "burning up all aesthetics" is related to his critique of what he was later to call the "retinal" (as explained above); but the idea of an artwork figuring the possible as such, and giving it a determined form, is common to all artworks produced with no consideration for the status of the artist, for the reception, acceptance or rejection of the artwork.

The Pathological and the Obsessional

The celibate machine produces vibration, tension; it produces desire, so to speak, in a pure state. As Peter Gorsen wrote in the catalogue for the "Celibate Machines" exhibition, sexual obsessions have very often taken the form of machinic dispositives in the history of Western iconography:

> The construction of very complex mechanical dispositives is also sought in order to bestow the fantasy of power the most fantastic form. In the exaggeration and excessiveness lies the very meaning of sexual obsession. The optimal relation between excitement and reaction is the *detour* through a very precise motor mechanism comprising the greatest possible number of intermediary elements. [...] Marcel Duchamp is the uncontested master of this paradoxical strategy of complication that one finds in realms as diverse as torture devices from the Middle Ages, fetishist drawings of neurotics and schizophrenics (cf. for example Robert Gie, Heinrich Anton Müller, and in literature, Artaud, Schreber), and the technological fantasizing of science fiction.[30]

If we set apart the fact that Gorsen's approach puts an exaggerated accent on the sexual dimension, his interpretation is nevertheless precious because he builds a link between Duchamp's machine and the works of famous 'outsiders' (Robert Gie and Heinrich Anton Müller), both exhibited by Harald Szeemann in 1975.[31] This link is due not to a pathology, but rather to a certain structure of subjectivity: a solitude grappling with the power of desire. Gorsen insists on the masturbatory dimension of the celibate machine as a representation of the irreducible solitude of the desiring subject. My claim is paradoxical, that this very representation is at the same time, a negative appeal to a form of primal sociality, a kind of *infra*subjective relationality. Not an actual relation with real others, but rather the condition of a possibility of a relation, i. e. the internal tension towards the other known as desire, but in a pure state, without the actual presence of the other. Duchamp's work, along with many works of 'outsiders,' is thus paradoxically an affirmation of the sociality of any sub-

30 Peter Gorsen, in Szeemann and Clair 1975, p. 136 (my translation, from the French).

31 Both belong to the collection of the Musée de l'Art Brut in Lausanne.

jectivity inasmuch as its fundamental feature is that of tending towards the other, just as the bachelors are tending towards the bride.

References

Alliez, E. 2013, *Défaire l'image. De l'art contemporain*, in: collaboration with J.-C. Bonne, Les Presses du réel, Dijon.

Barr Jr, A. H. 1936, *Fantastic Art, Dada, Surrealism*, exhibition catalogue, Museum of Modern Art, New York.

Carrouges, M. 1976, *Les machines célibataires,* Chêne, Paris [1st ed.: 1954].

Clair, J. 1975, *Marcel Duchamp ou le grand fictif,* Galilée, Paris.

Clair, J. 2000, *Sur Marcel Duchamp et la fin de l'art,* Gallimard, Paris.

Deleuze, G. and Guattari, F. 1983, *Anti-Oedipus. Capitalism and Schizophrenia,* Minnesota University Press, Minneapolis.

Dubuffet, J. 1967, *Prospectus et tous écrits suivants,* t. 1, Gallimard, Paris.

Duchamp, M. 1973, *Salt Seller: The Essential Writings of Marcel Duchamp,* Oxford University Press, New York; trans. from Duchamp du signe, eds. M. Sanouillet and P. Matisse, Flammarion, Paris 2008 [last edition].

Duchamp, M. 2009, *Etant donnés,* ed. M. Taylor, Yale University Press, New Haven.

Duchamp, M. 2014, *Entretiens avec Pierre Cabanne,* Allia, Paris [1st ed.: 1967]

Egenhofer, S. 2010, *Produktionsästhetik,* Diaphanes, Zurich.

Jones, A. 1994, *Postmodernism and the En-gendering of Marcel Duchamp,* Cambridge University Press, New York.

Lageira, J. 2013, *Regard oblique. Essais sur la perception*, La Lettre Volée, Bruxelles.

Lazzarato M. 2014, *Marcel Duchamp et le refus du travail,* Les Prairies ordinaires, Paris.

Maldiney, H. 2007, *Penser l'homme et la folie,* Jérôme Millon, Grenoble.

Marcadé, B. 2007, *Marcel Duchamp. La vie à credit,* Flammarion, Paris.

Merleau-Ponty, M. 1964, *Sense and Non-Sense,* trans. H. J. Dreyfus and P. A., Dreyfus. Northwestern University Press, Evanston (IL).

Paz, O. 1990, *Marcel Duchamp: Appearance Stripped Bare,* Arcade Publishing, New York.

Prinzhorn, H. 2011, *Artistry of the Mentally Ill. A Contribution to the Psychology and Psychopathology of Configuration,* Springer, New York, trans. E. von Brockdorff from *Bildnerei der Geisteskranken. Ein Beitrag zur Psychologie und Psychopathologie der Gestaltung,* Springer Verlag, Berlin-Heidelberg 1922 [1st ed.: 1972]

Szeemann, H. and Clair J. 1975, *Junggesellenmaschinen/Les machines célibataires.* Exhibition catalogue, Alfieri, Venice.

Szeemann, H. 1981, *Museum der Obsessionen,* Merve Verlag, Berlin.

Szeemann, H., Bezzola, T. and Kurzmeyer R. (eds.) 2007, *Harald Szeemann with by through because towards despite. Catalogue of all Exhibitions 1957–2005,* Springer, Vienna, New York.

5

Animating Ideas:
Pathology and the Aesthetic Idea in Kant and Deleuze

Louis Schreel

> Spiritual entities or abstract ideas are not what we think they are: they are emotions or affects.
> —Gilles Deleuze, *The Shame and the Glory: T. E. Lawrence*

There is a strange analogy between Kant's and Deleuze's accounts of aesthetic contemplation. In both cases we are dealing with a vitalist theory of forces, a dynamist interpretation of aesthetic feeling as an augmentation of the spectator's vital feeling, of what Kant calls our *Lebensgefühl.* Kant calls the principle that increases life force *Geist,* which the most recent English translation of the third *Critique* translates as "spirit," since its function is to *animate.* Within Kant's subject-oriented paradigm, this enlivening principle frees our state of mind from its "pathological" subordination to desires and other empirical interests and directs it to the super-sensible, which Kant determines as the *idea* that transcends all sensibility. As one will remember, for Kant the intensity of the pleasure of aesthetic contemplation can never be understood as merely sensory: it presupposes a special "disposition" (*Stimmung*) that goes beyond empirical interests. What is at stake in beautiful art is not the sensible presentation (*sinnliche Darstellung*) but an intensive intuition that is imported, through an imaginative transformation, from the bodily to the spiritual, an "ennoblement and elevation" above one's mere receptivity for pleasure or displeasure from sensible impressions (Kant 2000, pp. 227, 110).[1]

---

[1] Although Kant uses the term "contemplation" for judgments of beauty in both nature and art, as also for the sublime, I shall restrict my focus here to how contemplation results from the expression of aesthetic ideas in art, leaving a consideration of how ideas animate the mind contemplating nature for another occasion.

For Deleuze, Kant's most important insight remains that by isolating art from practical interests and thereby from empirical reality he has indicated its essential moment in the negation of reality itself. Like Kant, Deleuze's account of contemplation invokes a *spiritual* enlivening principle which animates our faculties by directing them at an idea that pushes our sensibility (the faculty of being affected) toward a transcending and transcendental transgression of its lower empirical exercise. That which is sensed frees the imagination from its reproductive (*mnesic*) function within the representational logic of recognition and pushes it toward a properly productive, creative exercise, which, in turn, forces the understanding to think that which in extension lies beyond its concepts, giving "much food for thought" (Deleuze 2011, p. 188). The Kantian nature of this thought I believe is immediately clear: art animates the mind by means of ideas. It seems one cannot neglect this analogy with Kant's theory of aesthetic ideas to understand how for Deleuze art can *block* our speculative and pragmatic interests and open up the broader experiential basis of our cognitive and existential relation to the world.

However, there is an important difference between a mood which, in Kant's view, speaks in the name of human reason and a vital sensation which, in Deleuze's eyes, is the manifestation of the animalistic roots of reason. For Kant the aesthetic idea, as the enlivening principle of aesthetic delight, allows one to get in touch with the super-sensible substratum of the intellectual faculties, the "soul" in which all the faculties are said to converge and which transcends all sensibility, even the sensibility transformed by the imagination. This determination of the aesthetic idea implies that the increased vital feeling concerns for Kant first and foremost the spiritual life of the *Gemüt* and its principal *detachment* from the pathological life of instincts, drives, emotions and desires. For Deleuze, however, the aesthetic idea manifests a different kind of "beyond" of the pleasure principle, one which concerns exclusively the *passivity* of one's sensibility and which opens up the lived reality of a sub-representational domain. Aligning himself with a tradition coming from Plotinus through Leibniz and Hume up to Whitehead, Deleuze, with Guattari, opposes his vitalism to that of Kant:

> Vitalism has always had two possible interpretations: that of *an Idea that acts*, but is not—that acts therefore only from the point of view of an external cerebral knowledge (from Kant to Claude Bernard); or that of *a force that is but does not act*—that is therefore a pure internal Awareness (from Leibniz to Ruyer). If the second interpretation seems to us to be imperative it is because the contraction that preserves is always in a state of detachment in relation to action or even to movement and appears as a pure contemplation without knowledge. This can be seen even in the cerebral domain par excellence of apprenticeship or the formation of habits: although everything seems to take place by active connections and progressive integrations, from one test to another, the tests or cases, the occurrences, must, as Hume showed, be contracted in a contemplating 'imagination' while remaining distinct in relation to actions and to knowledge (Deleuze & Guattari 1994, p. 213, my emphasis).

If one wishes to address the dualism between Kant's and Deleuze's vitalist conceptions of aesthetic ideas one can best turn to Hume, to whom Deleuze dedicates his first study and whose theory of the instinctive roots of reason is applied in *Difference and Repetition* to develop a materialist resourcing of Kant's theory of ideal animation. In this essay, I will focus in particular on Deleuze's reading of Hume's theory of the imagination as an animalistic power of contraction that is constitutive of ideas. It will be argued that one should favor this model of a sub-representational, non-egological power of contraction over Kant's theory of productive imagination to account for Deleuze's conception of the animating function of aesthetic ideas. On this account the aesthetic idea will be caught up in an unlimited, a-rational becoming, a discontinuous distribution of intensive energy, which is at odds with the way in which Kant understands the participation in ideal sense. That is to say, in Kant's idealist theory of the ends of reason the idea finds its origin within subjectivity alone: ideas are always generated in accordance with the principles of the cognitive faculties (Kant 2000, pp. 218–219). In Deleuze's materialist theory of the animalistic roots of reason, on the contrary, the idea is grounded in an extra-subjective element which does not belong to the register of consciousness—at most a very rudimentary, morphodynamic form of consciousness, as Deleuze puts it on some occasions.[2] While for Kant, despite the sensory origin of the aesthetic idea, one must conceive *all* ideas (both aesthetic and intellectual) as spiritual entities that *act* in the mind *without* existing materially—that act therefore from a purely human or divine point of view of an external cerebral cognition, for Deleuze and Hume the exact opposite must be considered, even if for an idealist philosophy it means total heresy of the spirit: in their primitive birthing, ideas originate as spatio-temporal dynamisms that *coexist* with matter and that *receive* its movements from within.

This means that in Deleuze's account of the aesthetic idea the art contemplator will not "perceive" matter—as in Kant's theory of the productive imagination which "forms" matter by analogies and the understanding recognizing the remodeled matter—but rather the spectator will sense within herself an instinctive, libidinal form of intelligence that interacts with matter without differing from it, like the Kantian soul differs from matter. The difference between Kant's and Deleuze's conceptions of the vitality of aesthetic contemplation concerns precisely the fact that for Kant the liveliness does not designate a sensation of life in the biological sense, while for Deleuze it does. In Deleuze's view, ideal sense arises already at the level of biological individuation, particularly in the genesis of organic functions.[3] The aesthetic inten-

---

2 See for example: Deleuze & Guattari 1994, pp. 212–213; Deleuze 1994, p. 220.

3 An account of biological individuation, particularly of the genesis of organic functions, in terms of morphodynamic ideas can be found in: Deleuze 1994, chap. 4.

sification of the sub-representational dimension of sensation is for Deleuze closely connected to the resurrection of an instinctive, animalistic form of "pure internal Awareness," a "soul" that can be ascribed to all living entities and that Kant reserves for the human and supra-human only (Deleuze & Guattari 1994, pp. 211, 213).

1. Kant on the Spirit as the Animating Principle in the Mind

1.1 The *Gemüt*

From the first paragraph of the third *Critique* onward Kant explains he will conceive the delight that a representation provides for thought by referring it wholly to the subject, and more specifically to its "feeling of life" (*Lebensgefühl* (Kant 2000, p. 90, Kant 1974, p. 40)). He calls pleasure an increase of the vital force and displeasure the reduction of this force. The above-mentioned definition of the spirit (*Geist*) as the animating principle in the mind is given in paragraph forty nine on the faculties of the mind that constitute artistic genius:

> *Spirit [Geist]*, in an aesthetic significance, means the animating *[belebende]* principle in the mind *[Gemüte]*. That, however, by which this principle animates the soul *[Seele]*, the material *[Stoff]* which it uses for this purpose, is that which purposively sets the mental powers *[die Gemütskräfte]* into motion, i. e. into a play that is self-maintaining and even strengthens the powers to that end (Kant 2000, p. 192; Kant 1974, p. 167).

One is struck to find in this passage a confusing combination of terms—*Geist, Gemüt, Seele*—without any reference to the subject *(Subjekt)* itself, which the first paragraph had said to focus on. In fact, the concept designating subjectivity is that of the *Gemüt* or mind, which the first *Critique* defined as "the inner sense, by means of which the mind intuits itself, or its inner state" (Kant 1998, p. 157).[4] The function

---

4 In the context of the third *Critique* the term *"Gemüt"* refers primarily to the apprehension of an affective correlate without cognitive content. Given the corporeal connotations of the original German term, I will use "*Gemüt*" instead of "mind" in the following.

of the *Gemüt* is to enable by means of a series of time-syntheses a unified intuition of its inner state. The *Gemüt* is the transcendental, *a priori* temporal form "under which the intuition of its inner state is alone possible" (Kant 1998, p. 157). As the act of representation in intuition, it can take on a variety of modes, depending on whether one "intuits," "conceives," forms a "notion," or an "idea."

We have already noted that aesthetic contemplation is only possible for Kant when the *Gemüt* takes on a very specific disposition *(Stimmung)*, namely one in which it is emptied of desires, cognitive contents, passions, moral or political engagements and other forms of interest. Contemplation is *interesselose Wohlgefallen.* In aesthetic judgments, the *Gemüt* not only has no cognitive interest, but also senses something without any exercise of the will: it is emptied of both sensible attraction (an empirical, "pathological" interest in the existence of the object of sensation) and intellectual inclination (a pure practical interest in the existence of an object of the will).[5] Accordingly, when Kant speaks in the above-cited passage of the mental powers *(Gemütskräfte)*, he is referring to a state of mind in which the *Gemüt* accounts *only* for an emotional apprehension.

But, Kant says, contemplation must be distinguished from emotion. For emotion *(Rührung)* is a sensation in which the movement of the soul is produced only by means of a momentary inhibition and followed by a stronger outpouring of the vital force (Kant 2000, p. 111). This structure of emotion belongs to sublimity and not to beauty, because the latter happens *immediately* while the former always takes

[5] I follow here the distinction made in Kant's *First Introduction* to the third *Critique* between the faculty of cognition, the feeling of pleasure and displeasure and the faculty of desire, which are said to make up the three fundamental faculties of the human mind. See: Kant 2000, p. 11. As we will see, Deleuze's account of the aesthetic idea will reintroduce the will into contemplation, albeit in an impersonal form.

places in different steps that mediate it. The sublime, unlike beauty, is quasi-dialectical: for the life forces to increase our cognitive efforts at comprehension must first collide. Only the enigmatic moment of apprehending something *ungraspable*, which induces a contra-purposive, qualitative *leap* with regard to the laws of representation, can *à la limite* animate the powers of the *Gemüt*. This is why Deleuze is closer to Kant's conception of sublime emotion than beauty when he says in an interview with the French newspaper *Le Monde* (on his Bacon study) that the structure of emotion cannot be understood as a reflective self-presence. Emotion always implies a certain division in the self, a polarity between that which is sensed and one's comprehension. As he puts it:

> Emotion does not say "I". You said it yourself: you are beside yourself. Emotion is not of the order of the ego but of the event. It is very difficult to grasp an event, but I do not believe that this grasp implies the first person (Deleuze 2007, p. 187).

Unlike this tumultuous character of emotion, beauty induces an *immediate* and *calm* increase of the vital force.

In sum, although it is emptied of cognitive and pragmatic interests, the contemplative *Gemüt* faced with beauty still appears to be affective, but *only* insofar as it is turned inward, toward the calm, purposive and disinterested interaction of its cognitive powers. As we will see, with Deleuze's account of contemplation, this specific disposition *(Stimmung)* essential to contemplation will take on a different structure, closer to that of emotion, and a form of time that has broken with a temporality of linear succession which distributes moments centered on the present instant. But before going into Deleuze's modification of Kant's model, let us first further our consideration of the Kantian principle of animating ideas.

1.2 The Spiritual Life of the *Gemüt*

To get an accurate view on the relation between the *Gemüt*, and *Geist* as the principle of growth of the vital force "in" the *Gemüt*, we must look at precisely what kind of life is at stake here. At the end of the exposition of aesthetic reflective judgments and just before proceeding to their deduction, Kant distinguishes his recourse to the vitalist motif from Burke's vitalism in the *Enquiry*. Kant grants Burke the value of an empirical survey of the realm of psycho-physiological phenomena, as also his need of using vitalism to explain these realities. The passage reads as follows:

> As Epicurus maintained, gratification and pain are always ultimately corporeal, whether they originate from the imagination or even from representations of the understanding: because life without the feeling of the corporeal organ is merely consciousness of one's existence, but not a feeling of well- or ill-being, i. e., the promotion or inhibition of the powers of life; because the mind [*Gemüt*] for itself is entirely life (the principle of life itself [*das Lebensprinzip selbst*]), and hindrances or promotions must be sought outside it, though in the human being himself, hence in combination with his body (Kant 2000, pp. 158–159).

Although Kant does grant that all pleasure and displeasure, all gratification and pain, involve the feeling of a living entity in the biological sense—a corporeal, organic being—it becomes quickly clear that the feeling of life involved in aesthetic contemplation concerns a different form of life: the spiritual life of the *Gemüt*. Surely all feeling of life (no matter how intellectual or cerebral) requires a bodily basis and can accordingly always be evaluated in terms of a hindrance or promotion of the vital forces. But the "feeling of the promotion of life" (Kant 2000, p. 128) that is "directly" brought about in aesthetic contemplation concerns (first and foremost) the life of the *Gemüt* and not (exclusively) that of the body. It surely has an irreducible bodily, material dimension but concerns primarily the *Gemüt's* capacity of self-affection, which in turn presupposes subjectivity. As Jan Völker notes, the feeling of life sensed in aesthetic contemplation is to be understood on the background of

Kant's distinction between "the immaterial [...] *principium* of life" and the "material," which runs parallel to the distinction between "automaton" and "spirit."[6] For Kant, spiritual life "starts from the death of the animal" and must thus be clearly distinguished from the teleologically defined organic life in nature (the capacity of a corporeal being to be cause and effect of its own activity).[7] These two forms of life are not thought of as being in continuity, as empiricists like Hume and Deleuze do, but as two separate and opposed realms: spiritual life is *cultural*, it is the product of an individual and collective intentionality. For Kant, animals cannot appreciate art because this requires the capacity to consider something as an end *in itself*, independent of needs centered on the present moment: art is *Zweckmäßigkeit ohne Zweck*.[8] This distinction concerns precisely the fact that the *spiritual* principle that animates the *Gemüt* does so by means of *ideas* and not by sensory impressions only. In terms of Kant's distinction between agreeableness (a satisfaction that is pathologically conditioned by sensory stimuli) and beauty (a merely contemplative, disinterested satisfaction), the first is also valid for non-rational animals, while contemplation is "valid only for human beings, i. e., animal but also rational beings, but not merely as the latter (e. g. spirits), rather as beings who are at the same time animal" (Kant 2000, p. 95). We will retain here for now that the spirit's function is first of all to

6 Immanuel Kant, *Notes and Fragments*, trans. Curtis Bowman, Paul Guyer, and Frederick Rauscher, ed. Paul Guyer (New York: Cambridge University Press, 2005), p. 88 (Reflection 3855, 1764–1768). Cited in: Völker 2009, p. 67.

7 Immanuel Kant, *Handschriftlicher Nachlaß Metaphysik*, part I, *Kant's gesammelte Schriften*, Published by The Royal Prussian Academy of Sciences, vol. XVII, Handwritten *Nachlaß* Metaphysics (Berlin and Leipzig: de Gruyter, 1926), p. 474, R 4240. (1 (?) 1769–1770). Cited in: Völker 2009, p. 67.

8 On the side of artistic production, Kant claims in § 43 that for an activity to count as art the agent must have consciously conceived a determinate concept of the product, *as an end*, which he calls a "production through freedom, i. e. through a capacity for choice that grounds its actions in reason," and not just produce something through instinct, like bees making a honeycomb (Kant 2000, pp. 182–183).

awaken in the *Gemüt*, as the passive site of empirical determination, *its receptivity to ideas*. Let us consider now how the spirit animates the *Gemüt*.

1.3 The Aesthetic Idea

In the quoted passage on the spirit, Kant specifies that the enlivening principle in the mind animates the powers by means of a productive dynamism of the imagination. Beyond its empirical use in cognition (the schematism), the imagination is said to have also the more "original" task of animating the faculties by directing them at the super-sensible, which Kant determines as the idea that transcends all sensibility. In its empirical use, the latter is under the constraint of the understanding and is subject to the limitation of being adequate to its concepts. Yet, in its aesthetic use, the imagination is free from conceptual constraints and spontaneously provides unsought, extensive and undeveloped material for thought (*ungesucht, reichhaltigen Stoff für den Verstand* (Kant 2000, p. 194; Kant 1974, pp. 171–172)) of which the understanding took no regard in its concept, but which it applies, "not so much objectively, for cognition, as subjectively, for the animation of the cognitive powers" (*zur Belebung der Erkenntniskräfte* (Kant 2000, p. 194; Kant 1974, p. 172)). Kant calls this animating principle of the imagination "the faculty for the presentation of aesthetic ideas" (*das Vermögen der Darstellung ästhetischer Ideen* (Kant 2000, p. 192; Kant 1974, p. 167)).

It is this animation, this affective dynamism of the imagination, that comes to the fore as the "feeling of life" in aesthetic, reflecting judgments. The aesthetic idea—whose expression constitutes beautiful art—is an essential component of aesthetic judgment, allowing the spectator to go from an intensive, sensory impression to a reflection of the broader experiential *basis* of her cognitive and existential relation to the world. Other than a pure concept, the aesthetic idea produces in the spectator the intuition of *another nature* than the one that is given to her. Kant calls the aesthetic ideas also "secondary representations" *(Nebenvorstellungen)* of the imagination that give "much to think," "though without it being possible for any determinate thought, i. e. concept, to be adequate to it, which, consequently, no language fully attains or can make intelligible" (Kant 2000, p. 192; Kant 1974, p. 168). Contrary to the ideas of reason, these are intuitions (of the imagination) beyond conceptual grasp. But just like the intellectual ideas they manifest reason's "restless striving" toward something lying beyond the bounds of experience (cf. Kant 1998, p. 110). This striving is properly speaking metaphysical because the imagination, Kant writes, is "very powerful in creating, as it were, another nature, out of the material which the real one gives it" (Kant 2000, p. 192). In fact, Kant says that the imagination strives toward precisely an approximate *intuitive* presentation of intellectual ideas, which gives them the *appearance* of an objective reality:

> The poet ventures to make sensible rational ideas of invisible beings, the kingdom of the blessed, the kingdom of hell, eternity, creation, etc., as well as to make that of which there are examples in experience, e. g., death, envy, and all sorts of vices, as well as love, fame, etc., sensible beyond the limits of experience, with a completeness that goes beyond anything of which there is an example in nature, by means of an imagination that emulates the precedent of reason in attaining to a maximum (Kant 2000, pp. 192–193).

We can see in this passage that aesthetic ideas cannot be reduced to the sensible presentation of intellectual ideas alone. Kant distinguishes within the presentational content of aesthetic ideas between two categories: intellectual ideas and what Samantha Matherne calls "experience-oriented aesthetic ideas" (Matherne 2012, p. 9). The intellectual ideas category designates ideas that have no objective correlate in experience. These are the kinds of ideas that the previous *Critiques* had said to spring from reason: the theoretical ideas of God, the soul and the world-whole in the first *Critique*, and the moral ideas of the moral law, virtue and freedom in the second *Critique*.

The experience category, on the other hand, are aesthetic ideas that are oriented primarily toward objects of ordinary experience—such as love, death, envy, fame etc.—and not toward objects that we could never, in principle, experience (such as God, the soul etc.). But why call the artistic presentation of these objects *ideas?* Unlike rational ideas, aesthetic ideas originate in a sensible faculty (imagination), but they remain *ideas* because even they must first of all be representations of a totality, that is, of unity in diversity. For Kant they count as ideas precisely insofar that they present the example drawn from experience "with a completeness" that goes beyond the limits of ordinary experience (Kant 2000, p. 192). As Matherne puts it: "After all, our own experience of art tells us that many artists do not aim at capturing something we cannot experience, but rather bringing to light the richness of experience we too often overlook in the exigencies of everyday life" (Matherne 2012, pp. 9–10). Consider the following passage from D. H. Lawrence's *Women in Love:*

> All the world was lapsing into a grey wish-wash of nothingness, she had no contact and no connexion anywhere. She despised and detested the whole show. From the bottom of her heart, from the bottom of her soul, she despised and detested people, adult people. [...]
> She could be very pleasant and flattering, almost subservient, to people she met. But no one was taken in. Instinctively each felt her contemptuous mockery of the human being in himself, or herself. She had a profound grudge against the human being. That which the word "human" stood for was despicable and repugnant to her.
> Mostly her heart was closed in this hidden, unconscious strain of contemptuous ridicule. She thought she loved, she thought she was full of love. This was her idea of herself. But the strange brightness of her presence, a marvelous radiance of intrinsic vitality, was a luminousness of supreme repudiation, nothing but repudiation.
> Yet, at moments, she yielded and softened, she wanted pure love, only pure love. This other, this state of constant unfailing repudiation, was a strain, a suffering also. A terrible desire for pure love overcame her again (Lawrence 1960, pp. 275–276).

In isolating the sense connected to the everyday experience of love, Lawrence circles around a region of sense that is not accessible through an extensional, representational use of language where words are thought of as functioning to call together an ensemble of existing objects that are its reference. In this conception of language words are supposed to refer to an extra-linguistic state of affairs. But writing about Ursula Brangwen's (im)possibility for love, Lawrence is not designating the class of existing relationships or situations in which love is actualized. In the phrase "a terrible desire for love overcame her again," the term "love" is not used as a proper name designating an item in reality or a class of beings or state of affairs. Rather, "love" is here an idea covering a region of sense that sollicitates to be *created.* Unlike the proper name "Ursula Brangwen," which refers and corresponds to a singular, distinct and determinate object as its fixed referent, the sense of an idea is not an object, nor a plurality of objects, but it is an unsaturated function, an incompleteness that waits upon determinate incarnations that actualize it.

On a Kantian analysis, Lawrence introduces love as something familiar to us from experience. Upon reading the concept "love" we spontaneously interpret it *like* a concept referring to something with a fixed meaning. But as he goes on he presents this concept of love through an aesthetic idea filled with "aesthetic attributes" (Kant 2000, p. 193) involving metaphorical descriptions of "the marvelous radiance" and "brightness of her presence." And as these attributes present Ursula's impossibility of the concept of love, being attached and compromised by a profound repudiation which shines through to others around her, although without her being aware of it, Lawrence extends the familiarity of the example beyond its conceptual limits, hence past the bounds of our ordinary experience. The sense in "play" in the aesthetic experience is not understood as the mode of presentation of an extra-linguistic object but rather it isolates and directs us to the function of the productive imagination to *create* sense, to engage reality in a symbolically meaningful way. And it does so in a way that fleshes out the fragile nature of this kind of *ideal* sense production, its way of escaping the fixed, logical grasp of our understanding's generalities, thus giving "much food for thought."

It is important to note that on Kant's account an aesthetic idea giving a beautiful *expression* of an emotion like love cannot in turn induce an emotion on the contemplator's side. Recall that contemplation presupposes self-*reflection* through a disinterested and purposive interplay between the imagination and understanding, while emotions are "affects" that arise immediately and suddenly as a response to a present situation, involving a surprise *through* sensation. A sudden feeling of fear, joy or sadness is a pathological affect, not a contemplation. Insofar as they arise immediately and through sensation alone, they are for Kant "unpremeditated," have no ground in thought and reflection and exclude thus a contemplative state (Kant 2000, p. 154).[9] Beautiful art may express the *fragility* of love but it should not express the *anarchy* of its sense (the anarchy of "the terrible desire"): the fact that sense is irreducible to the understanding's logical grasp may not be sensed as contra-final. Why is this the case? Because beautiful art must for Kant render sensible the subjective faculty of animating ideas in a way that is precisely not emotional but self-determining. What is crucial here for Kant is that even though the kind of thought that animates ideas always contains a *rebellious* element that is incomplete, an unsaturatedness that cannot be reduced to an object, at the same time all ideas are per-

[9] It should be noted that pathological affects do not exclude a sublime form of contemplation, because here reflection is said to arise *as a result* of the hampering of the freedom of the mind.

fectly determinable by means of a method that uses procedures *analogous* to those of cognition (the schematism) and at the disposal of which the intentional subject is, therefore, in control. It is this possibility and its fragility which, for Kant, beauty fleshes out. This begs the question: Does Lawrence's passage qualify as beautiful? The sequel of the passage is decisive:

> She went out one evening, numbed by this constant essential suffering. Those who are timed for destruction must die now. The knowledge of this reached a finality, a finishing in her. And the finality released her. If fate would carry off in death or downfall all those who were timed to go, why need she trouble, why repudiate any further? She was free of it all, she could seek a new union elsewhere (Lawrence 1960, p. 276).

1.4 Pathological Art

To return to our passage on the spirit, the imagination is said to animate the mental powers by presenting a material *(Stoff)* that is spiritualized. We have seen that this "presenting" or "giving" of material designates a *transformative* operation of the imagination which immediately induces a purposive play with the understanding, a vitalizing play that is self-maintaining. That which is formed and "given" to thought, the "material," designates always a manifold or multiplicity without order. For Kant it is not the material *itself* which induces this play, but only the fact that the productive imagination discovers within itself a finality concerning its *principal* autonomy from the material. By itself, the matter of sensation *(Materie der Empfindung)* attaches us to charm or emotion, orienting sensation toward mere enjoyment *(Genuss)*, "which leaves behind it nothing in the idea, and makes the spirit dull, the object by and by loathsome, and the mind, because it is aware that its disposition is contrapurposive *(zweckwidrigen Stimmung)* in the judgment of reason, dissatisfied with itself and moody" (Kant 2000, p. 203). Nonetheless, when considering artistic practice as a transformation of a material object into an artistic object, Kant considers the materiality of the object as a necessary *constraint* to the play of the faculties:

> It is not inadvisable to recall that in all liberal arts there is nevertheless required something compulsory, or as it is called, a mechanism, without which the spirit, which must be free in the art and which alone animates the work, would have no body at all and would entirely evaporate (Kant 2000, p. 183).

This compulsory dimension *(etwas Zwangmäßiges)* stems from the free materials of nature—colors, sounds—which in themselves are difficult to reflect for the imagination but *by means* of which nature and art produce objects that are apt to be reflected formally and procure the feeling of beauty. The material or *Stoff* does seem here to be that which induces movement into the *Gemüt*, throwing the cognitive faculties into a free play on the basis of bodily, psycho-physiological stimuli. But this is not *constitutive* of the feeling of beauty. The confusion arising here results from the fact that we have not yet taken into account the exact role of the imagination in the face of intuition. First of all, the compulsion must at all times be carefully balanced, composed, contained. Kant warns his readers:

> The combination and harmony of the two cognitive faculties, the sensibility and the understanding, which to be sure cannot manage without each other but which nevertheless cannot readily be united with each other without constraint and mutual harm, must seem to be unintentional and to happen on their own; otherwise it is not beautiful art (Kant 2000, p. 198).

And further on:

> In poetry, everything proceeds honestly and uprightly. It declares that it will conduct a merely entertaining play with the imagination, and indeed concerning form, in concord with the laws of the understanding, and does not demand that the understanding be deceived and embroiled through sensible presentation (Kant 2000, p. 205).

If the free materials of nature become too strongly accentuated, art tends toward a transgression of its merely *disinterested* aesthetic and contemplative function, thereby leading to what Kant would call a *pathological* art.[10] While the artist must have

[10] Kant does not explicitly speak of pathological art but rather of "agreeable rather than beautiful art." Unlike beautiful art which enlarges the faculties by awakening culture in the mind, an agreeable art is one that "merely plays with sensations" and is estimated according to its pathologically conditioned agreeableness. See for example: Kant 2000, p. 206.

spirit—i. e., the animating principle that provides rich material that escapes conceptual grasp—this must be counter-balanced with *disciplined* form-giving, an academic principle of "taste":

> Taste, like the power of judgment in general, is the discipline (or corrective) of genius, clipping its wings and making it well behaved or polished; but at the same time it gives genius guidance as to where and how far it should extend itself if it is to remain purposive; and by introducing clarity and order into the abundance of thoughts it makes the ideas tenable, capable of an enduring and universal approval, of enjoying a posterity among others and in an ever progressing culture (Kant 2000, p. 197).

The demand of restriction, of clipping the wings of genius and remaining in accordance with the laws of understanding expresses Kant's view that what is at stake in art is precisely not *sensible presentation (sinnliche Darstellung)*, but a sensory intuition that is imported, through an imaginative transformation, from the bodily to the spiritual, an "ennoblement and elevation" above the mere pathological receptivity for pleasure or displeasure from sensible impressions (Kant 2000, pp. 227, 110). The danger of deceiving *(überschleichen)* and embroiling *(verstricken)* through sensible presentation goes out from the material dimension of the work, which might address mainly the *passivity* of one's sensibility and divert the contemplator's attention to the actual existence of bodily, psycho-physiological stimuli, resulting in *mere* charm or emotion. In Kant's hierarchy of the arts, poetry is at the top, followed by oratory art, music, painting and finally sculpture and architecture, which are pathological ("agreeable") arts rather than truly beautiful arts because they are more bound to the sensible presentation and give a pathologically conditioned satisfaction.

For Kant, the sensible presentation itself is not *constitutive* of the aesthetic dimension. At the heart of his account of the aesthetic idea stands the productive imagination which grounds aesthetic contemplation in the subject's natural spontaneity to produce representations of an object *without* it being present in intuition. Recall that in the first *Critique*, Kant had defined the productive imagination as "the faculty for representing an object even without its presence in intuition" (Kant 1998, p. 256). This is the transcendental synthesis of the imagination, which must be distinguished from its empirical, "reproductive" synthesis, in which it forms a representation of an object we have previously intuited. The transcendental synthesis concerns a more fundamental act of formation—"an act of original formation *(Formung)*" as Cassirer puts it (Cassirer 1957, p. 134)—because it grounds the capacity that enables us to *detach* the intuited from the live experience, from the sensory present, and place it under the horizon of the concrete universality of time. This detachment from the present moment in which one remains immersed in things is, for Kant, a spontaneous way of immediately perceiving objects as meaningful wholes, still without and before recourse to discursive thought.[11] It is precisely this character—the subject's free and autonomous intentionality—that is put into *play* in aesthetic contemplation, namely its freedom from the limits of sensibility and its ability to *see* possibilities, its "ability to interchange present and nonpresent, the real and the possible," as Cassirer, again, puts it (Cassirer 1957, p. 315).[12]

In pathological experience, this transcendental function of the productive imagination is either absent or malfunctioning. This is why Herman Parret writes that the "degeneration or pathology of the aesthetic dimension can only be of the order of 'thymic disruptions', which Freud recognized but which have traditionally been neglected in patho-analysis. These disruptions are precisely pathologies that con-

[11] Whether or not Kant thought perception can occur through sensibility and imagination alone, without the influence of the understanding, is still a matter of debate.

[12] I rely here for Cassirer's reading of Kant's theory of productive imagination on Samantha Matherne's insightful article: "The Kantian Roots of Merleau-Ponty's Account of Pathology," *British Journal for the History of Philosophy*, vol. 22, no. 1 (2014), pp. 124–149 (pp. 130–131).

cern the faculty of temporalization, like depression and neurasthenia" (Parret 1988, p. 223).[13] In pathology, for example in depression, one has enormous difficulties to introduce oneself in the temporal cyclicality. For someone with depression the access to beauty—to "the cycle of time" as Parret puts it (Parret 1988, p. 223)—is therefore made impossible. But this does *not* amount to a total loss of intentionality, a total destruction of all vectors of meaning. In pathological disruptions of the aesthetic dimension the patient's perception is more restricted, but these disruptions do not lead to madness or a total extinction of self-consciousness itself, as in the case of psychosis.

Let us conclude. We have seen that for Kant, the self's base, pathological attachment to drives, instincts, emotions and desires can as such not be tolerated in the beautiful arts: the pathological must be lifted to the purely spiritual freedom of the mind, directing us to something "quite different from life," something much more worthy than life and its pathological "enjoyment" (cf. Kant 1996, p. 211). In Deleuze's materialist resourcing of Kant's aesthetics, however, aesthetic contemplation will be *inextricably* connected to a resurrection of the pathological, the animalistic, and at times even the psychotic experience of an organ-less and image-less body. It should be noted, however, that such an aesthetics of pathological art does not degrade art to the level of the culture industry directed only at the *sensational,* the constant induction of empirical stimuli of the agreeable. Deleuze maintains the Kantian emancipation of art—its autonomy—from the empirical, but from his point of view Kant's principle of disinterestedness rests on an illegitimate formal idealization of

13 Parret 1988, p. 223: "la dégénération ou la pathologie de la dimension esthétique ne peut être que de l'ordre des *perturbations thymiques*, reconnues par Freud bien que traditionnellement négligées en patho-analyse. Ces perturbations sont précisément des pathologies qui concernent la faculté de temporalisation, comme la dépression (dont Freud ne parle à peu près jamais, il faut l'admettre) et la neurasthénie" (my translation).

the imagination's ascribed reflective *autonomy*. As we will see, Deleuze converts this principle: insofar as aesthetic contemplation rests on the faculty of transcending the empirical, it directs us not to an *autonomous* spontaneity but rather to a faculty of transcending the given *without* being entirely *detached* from it.

2. Deleuze's Energetic Account of the Aesthetic Idea

2.1 The Rebellious Matter of Sensation

Deleuze's account of the aesthetic idea can be found in the middle of the third chapter of *Difference and Repetition* and exposes, as with Kant, the animating movement of an idea from sensibility to thought. The Kantian *Stoff* or material by means of which the soul is animated (the aesthetic idea) is said to be the object of a fundamental *encounter*. As with Kant, that which is encountered belongs always first and foremost to the domain of sensibility, yet unlike Kant it can be *grasped* only in a variety of affective, emotional tones: wonder, love, hatred, suffering (Deleuze 1994, p. 139). In whichever tone, its primary characteristic is that it can *only* be sensed and *never* be *recognized*. Unlike Kant's requirement of an *immediate* purposive communication between the different cognitive faculties, Deleuze stresses the violent character of the experience, "the claws of a strangeness or an enmity" inherent to the shock that forces the intimacy of thought to abandon its "natural stupor," its merely abstract possibilities (Deleuze 1994, p. 140). "Sensibility," Deleuze writes, "in the presence of that which can only be sensed […] finds itself before its own limit […] and raises itself to the level of a transcendent exercise" (Deleuze 1994, p. 140). As we will see, this *transcendent* exercise, which coincides with its transcendental exercise, concerns a creative exercise of the imagination's power of contraction that is constitutive of the most primitive form of ideality: *drives* or *habits*. Before going into the role of the imagination in sensation, however, let us look into the other two characteristics of the animation of thought.

The second characteristic of the encounter is that it "moves the soul, 'perplexes' it—in other words, forces it to pose a problem: as though the object of encounter, the sign, were the bearer of a problem—as though it were a problem" (Deleuze 1994, p. 140). This second characteristic concerns the fact that the encounter that gives rise to the genesis of ideas does not lead to the harmonious exercise of the faculties of the soul, as in the case of the recognition of an object. That the idea is sensed as *problematic* means it does not merely *thwart* conceptual identification, as in the Kantian beautiful, but that it *exceeds* both the imagination's faculty of presentation and the understanding's recognition. The encounter is a kind of qualitative "leap" which introduces "unsettling difficulties" into the "sedentary structures of representation" (Deleuze 1994, p. 37). The third characteristic, finally, is that the encounter passed on from sensibility to imagination in turn forces thought to grasp that which can only be thought, "not the intelligible, for this is still no more than the mode in which we think that which might be something other than thought, but the being of the intelligible as though this were both the final power of thought and the unthinkable" (Deleuze 1994, p. 141).

Having outlined this schematic model of animation, Deleuze is quick to turn to Plato to point out the novelty of his conception of the encounter that forces thought to think. We have seen that the encounter does so by bringing each faculty of the soul to its "limit." Yet, the nature of this limit remains to be determined. Deleuze refers to a distinction Plato makes in *The Republic* between, on the one hand, (1) a dimension of fixity, measure and rest and, on the other hand, (2) an "unlimited qualitative becoming" "whose characteristic is to elude the present" and which constitutes the "sign or point of departure for that which forces thought" (Deleuze 1994, p. 141; Deleuze 1990, p. 1). As Deleuze writes in *The Logic of Sense*, returning again to the same passage in Plato:

> Plato invites us to distinguish two dimensions: (1) that of limited and measured things, of fixed qualities, permanent or temporary which always presupposes pauses and rests, the fixity of presents, and the assignation of subjects [...] and (2) a pure becoming without measure, a veritable becoming-mad, which never rests. It moves in both directions at once. It always eludes the present, causing future and past, more and less, too much and not enough to coincide in the simultaneity of a rebellious matter (Deleuze 1990, pp. 1–2).

Deleuze explains this measure-less becoming with an example of Socrates in the *Philebus* (24b-d), which concerns the traditional philosophical dissociation between the qualitative and the quantitative. The hotter and the colder, Socrates argues, cannot "take on a definite quality" since, as they are always "going a point further," they cannot stop and become fixed without becoming something other than themselves. This requires, for Socrates, that the qualitative—both the hotter and the colder—be characterized under the heading of the "unlimited" (ἄπειρον), as against the quantitative which is characterized, by contrast, by "limit" (πέρας) (Deleuze 1990, p. 2).

This dualism between the qualitative and the quantitative does for Deleuze not, however, concern the familiar opposition between the sensible and the intelligible, matter and Idea. Rather, it points to "a more profound and secret dualism hidden in sensible and material bodies themselves," namely between "that which *receives the action of the Idea and that which eludes this action*" (Deleuze 1990, p. 2, my emphasis). The rebellious matter of sensation is an unlimited becoming that eludes the limiting order and measure—that is to say: *resemblance*—which Ideas impose upon things. But inversely, it indicates for Deleuze a kind of (pro-)pulsive *force* of the material *(Stoff)* as such, an intensive energy underlying each quality and implicated within all *extensity.*[14] As we will see, Deleuze unlike Kant will hold the intensity of sensation itself to induce the animating, qualitative *leap* with regard to the laws of representational thought.

One can easily see in what sense Kant's conception of animation remains more indebted to the Platonic Idea: the intellect, as bearer of pure resemblance, projects the latter *(analogies of judgment, perceived resemblances, conceptual identity and conceptual opposition)* onto pure sensible diversity and the given rises from this encounter with matter. Accordingly, as we have seen, the aesthetic idea is for Kant always the product of a purposive inter*action* between forms of the imagination and categories of the understanding. Surely, that which forces thought to think (the aesthetic idea) is produced out of a play with the limits, the laws of the cognitive faculties which are imposed upon pure diversity, but this entertaining play is always *contained.* In Kant's Platonic form of contemplation the animation instantiated by the productive imagination cannot *exceed* the conceptual recognition—that is to say, the straightjacket of common sense—for otherwise *no* spiritual animation, no aesthetic pleasure can take place.

Now, it is essential to point out that Deleuze seeks to overturn exactly *this* account of ideal animation. There is no *"philia"* that testifies to "a good nature or good will by virtue of which the faculties would already possess or tend toward the object to which they are raised by violence, and by virtue of which they would enjoy an analogy with it or a homology among themselves" (Deleuze 1994, p. 145). "Even the point of departure—namely sensibility in the encounter with that which forces

[14] For Deleuze's refutation of the classical opposition between the qualitative and the quantitative see: Deleuze 1994, pp. 228–241.

sensation—presupposes neither affinity nor predestination" (Deleuze 1994, p. 145). For Deleuze, that which animates thought has nothing to do with either purposiveness *(Zweckmäßigkeit)* or a spontaneous form-giving faculty such as the Kantian productive imagination. The aesthetic idea becomes bound up with the unrepresentable and the task of art is precisely presentifying that which can never be totally grasped or recuperated conceptually. To be sure, however: "It is not the gods which we encounter: even hidden, the gods are only the forms of recognition. What we encounter are the demons, the sign-bearers: powers of the leap, the interval, the intensive and the instant; powers which only cover difference with more difference" (Deleuze 1994, p. 145).

Deleuze's account of the aesthetic idea begins with the conception of becoming as pure multiplicity deprived of resemblance—labeling it difference[15]—but refuses to install a transcendent counter-pole to becoming whose *actions*, that is to say, whose imposed limits, laws or principles of measurement would account for the genesis of ideas. He wants to take recourse to difference *only* to engender ideality.

2.2 Hume's Theory of Imagination as a Vital Force of Contraction

Let us, at this point, have a closer look at the passage by means of which we staged the dualism between the Kantian and Deleuzian vitalist conception of ideas:

> Vitalism has always had two possible interpretations: that of *an Idea that acts, but is not*—that acts therefore only from the point of view of an external cerebral knowledge (from Kant to Claude Bernard); or that of *a force that is but does not act*—that is therefore a pure internal Awareness (from Leibniz to Ruyer). If the second interpretation seems to us to be imperative it is because the contraction that preserves is always in a state of *detachment* in relation to action or even to movement and

[15] Cf. Deleuze 1994, p. 241: "a world *without identity*, without resemblance or equality, [...] a world the very ground of which is difference, in which everything rests upon disparities, upon differences of differences which reverberate to infinity (the world of intensity)."

> appears as a pure contemplation without knowledge. This can be seen even in the cerebral domain par excellence of apprenticeship or the formation of habits: although everything seems to take place by active connections and progressive integrations, from one test to another, the tests or cases, the occurrences, must, as Hume showed, be contracted in a contemplating 'imagination' while remaining distinct in relation to actions and to knowledge (Deleuze & Guattari 1994, p. 213, my emphasis). Chemical affinities and physical causalities themselves refer to primary forces capable of preserving their long chains by contracting their elements and by making them resonate: no causality is intelligible without this subjective instance. Not every organism has a brain, and not all life is organic but everywhere there are forces that constitute microbrains, or an inorganic life of things (Deleuze & Guattari 1994, pp. 212–213).

What to make of this conception of contemplation as the common root of the forces of nature and the drives of living organisms? What to make of the recourse to the Leibnizian *soul* or *force* (vis) which "preserves by contracting that which matter dissipates, or radiates, furthers, reflects, refracts, or converts" (Deleuze & Guattari 1994, p. 211)? First of all, one must leave behind the model of a mechanistic physics and opt for a dynamic physics which conceives of matter as energy and which explains nature and all movements of bodies in terms of two fundamental forces of attraction and repulsion.[16] Following Leibniz, Deleuze considers the essential state of matter as *mens momentanea*: each body is considered as a mind that is instantaneous but deprived of memory. For Leibniz, in fact, all material substances are quasi-living substances whose forces are nonetheless too bogged down in matter to be able to

[16] While in *Difference and Repetition* Deleuze is critical of Kant's conception of intensity in the first *Critique*, *Anti-Oedipus* values Kant's *Metaphysical Foundations of Natural Science* which conceives matter as being composed of two fundamental forces, one of repulsion, by means of which it fills space through infinite degrees and one of attraction, by means of which it acts in space through infinite degrees and at all distances (see *the Metaphysical Foundations of Dynamics*). The repulsive and attractive forces of matter constitute what Deleuze calls "intensive quantities," starting from intensity=0, which Deleuze calls the "body without organs" or a pure, unbound form of intensive energy. See: Deleuze & Guattari 2000, p. 19 and Montebello 2008, p. 186.

detach themselves and rise to the level of an autonomous psychic life.[17] To dispense all possible theological connotations, Deleuze defines the distribution of energy at this material level as obeying a "demonic rather than divine" principle:

> Here, there is no longer a division of that which is distributed but rather a division among those who distribute *themselves* in an open space—a space which is unlimited, or at least without precise limits. [...] It is an errant and even 'delirious' distribution, in which things are deployed across the entire extensity of a univocal and undistributed Being. It is not a matter of being which is distributed according to the requirements of representation, but of all things being divided up within being in the univocity of simple presence (the One-All). Such a distribution is demonic rather than divine (Deleuze 1994, pp. 36–37).

All (bio-)psychic and organic life—and with it the constitution of *lived time* ("duration")—emerges for Deleuze out of this chaotic distribution of energy by means of an elementary, vital synthetic power of contraction. Drawing on an essential thought of Hume's *Treatise*, Deleuze conceives the first level of psychic consistency as constituted by *habits*, which in turn consist of contracted expectations and pretentions. Only with the formation of a habit does something new—which was not given with matter itself—arise *in* the mind. This mind is not pre-given, but arises out of the collection of impressions which gives rise firstly to a number of expectations and secondly to habits. In its genesis the mind *is* nothing other than contemplation contracting habits. Out of the contraction of elements of matter we first have the birth of relatively simple expectations, which are like the building blocks of consciousness out of the pre-subjective realm of nature. As such, expectations and pretentions constitute the capacity to transcend what is directly present in matter and to *believe* that what

---

17 True mind, for Leibniz, is memory and anamnesis, continuous time. In other words: mind is matter that remembers its interactions, its immanence. But against the Cartesians, Leibniz argued that perception may very well occur without apperception or conscious reflection taking place. As he writes in a letter to Arnauld, such "quasi-perception is none other than the *expression* in a single indivisible being of divisible phenomena or of several beings." He adds to this that it must be shown that there are these "immaterial expressions which are without thought" not only in animals, but in living creatures such as vegetables, and even in bodily substances. Cited in: Lyotard 1988, p. 49 (my translation).

counts in it also belongs to the past or the future. In this sense expectation produces the present as a *lived* time (duration). Also, with the formation of expectations and beliefs arises the most primitive form of ideality. Belief, Hume says, is nothing other than a "lively idea": an imaginative activity in which what is not present is taken equally seriously (equally "lively") as what is present (Hume 1909, p. 396).[18]

The principle that permits us to extract from matter expectations about the future and to take the past into account is grounded in what Deleuze calls the imagination's power of *contraction*. As such, this contractile power consists in fusing *now* with *now* with *now* etc. Deleuze calls it a "sensitive plate" which "retains one case when the other appears": "it contracts cases, elements, agitations or homogeneous instants and grounds these in an internal qualitative impression endowed with a certain weight" (Deleuze 1994, p. 70). The imagination contracts the vibrations of matter and in so doing it constitutes its difference from it as a *lived* present. This does not yet presuppose memory or an operation of the understanding: "contraction is not a matter of reflection" (Deleuze 1994, p. 70). The contraction is not an *action* of an originary, constituent subjectivity but what Hume calls a *contemplation*: a *feeling* of the mind, a contemplation that preserves the before and the after.[19]

---

[18] For Hume all the perceptions of the mind are of two kinds, "viz. impressions and ideas, which differ only in their different degrees of force and vivacity" (Hume 1909, p. 396).

[19] Deleuze refers to Hume 1909, I, III, XIV (see: Deleuze & Guattari 1994, p. 212, p. 233, note 12). For Hume, the "uniting principle" among our inner perceptions is just as unintelligible as that among external objects, and "is not known to us in any other way than by experience," by "what we feel internally in contemplating" (Hume 1909, p. 463). Although Hume also calls the principle of forming beliefs and expectations *reason*, it is not at all to be confused with Descartes' or Kant's *ratio*, because it is at work also in irrational creatures such as animals, children and insane people. It is a kind of "animal reason," "a wonderful and unintelligible instinct in our souls" (Hume 1909, p. 471).

Deleuze explains this conception of the contractile imagination with Leibniz's concept of *mens momentanea* (Deleuze 1994, p. 70).[20] As noted, with Leibniz one must consider every material body as a mind that is instantaneous but deprived of memory. While we are beings with memories, there are also simple physical bodies without memory. At the moment when two bodies collide, they leave upon one another impressions of their motional tendencies, but these only last just as long as the transfer, which is instantaneous. In this sense physical bodies without memories are momentary minds, because none of the impressions that they receive will last for longer than an instant. This means also that momentary minds do not experience time as a continuous duration, like we usually do. For momentary minds there is just a "constantly aborted moment of birth" (Deleuze 1994, p. 70), a constant switch from given present nows that bear no temporal relations to other nows. Rather than live one constantly suspended now-moment, momentary minds live a constant intensive transition of collisions.

With Leibniz, Deleuze argues that the most rudimentary form of self-consciousness arises with the composition or contraction of momentary minds within a non-momentary mind, which Deleuze calls a "larval self" *(moi larvaire)*.[21] This composition consists in a contraction of material, successive instants into one internal qualitative impression endowed with a certain weight. As such, the larval contraction forms the most basic synthesis of time, which is also said to be the most primitive form of "spiritual" repetition in nature (Deleuze 1994, p. 25). Deleuze gives the example of

20 I follow here Corry Shores' insightful account of Deleuze's first time-synthesis in his article: "Self Shock: The Phenomenon of Personal Non-Identity in Inorganic Subjectivity" (Shores 2013).

21 Although the English translation of *Difference and Repetition* translates Deleuze's original term *"moi"* as "ego" ("a passive, partial, larval, contemplative and contracting ego" (Deleuze 1994, p. 97)), we prefer to use the term "self" because of the non-egological, passive nature ascribed to it by Deleuze.

the simplest cellular micro-organisms, which are composed of momentary minds (Deleuze 1994, p. 73). A cell, for example, might be composed of such elements as water, nitrogen, carbon and so on. Although cellular micro-organisms do not have an explicit awareness of time, the whole conglomeration has an undeniable primary vital sensibility. Each organism, in its receptive and perceptual elements, but also in its viscera, is to be considered as a sum of contractions, of retentions and expectations that allow it to act survivalistically, that is to say, to anticipate being a continuation of itself. In order to survive, the organism must have some kind of implicit knowledge that it has a past and a future, and thus it must constitute a past and a future in time, in the lived present, at the level of its primary vital sensibility.

For Deleuze, a cellular organism's genetic heritage can be said to be its awareness of the past, while its current *needs* are its awareness of the future. Clearly, the cell is not thinking about itself, but it does regard itself as a unity existing beyond the present. The past and the future belong to the single-cellular organism only *implicitly*: the past insofar as the preceding instants are retained in the contraction, the future because its expectation is anticipated in this same contraction. Past and future do not designate here instants *distinct* from an abstractly supposed present instant. Rather, they determine the dimensions of the present itself insofar as it is a contraction of instants. So although it is *constitutive* of lived time, the contraction is passive and not active because it is not carried out *by* the mind but occurs *in* the mind which contemplates purely in function of need, prior to all memory and all reflection.

But do we, beings with memories and complex cognitive faculties, not begin with determinate impressions and their faithful copies, the ideas or representations of them? For Deleuze and Hume, it would be a mistake to think so. In fact, all the perceptual syntheses we humans perform consciously are constituted upon such underlying, insensible and sub-representative organic syntheses which are like the sensibility *of* the senses. They refer back to a primary sensibility that we are: "We are made of contracted water, earth, light and air—not merely prior to the recognition or representation of these, but prior to their being sensed" (Deleuze 1994, p. 73). This brings with it a first important modification of Kant's theory of sensibility.

According to Deleuze, Kant's conception of receptivity defines the passive self in terms of the synthesis of apprehension in intuition *assuming* "sensations already formed, then merely relating these to the *a priori* forms of their representation which are determined as space and time" (Deleuze 1994, p. 98). Deleuze's "Transcendental Aesthetic," on the contrary, aims to account first for the constitution of the self and not directly for the world's constitution by the self: "the passive self is not defined simply by receptivity—that is, by means of the capacity to experience sensations—but by virtue of the contractile contemplation which constitutes the organism itself before it constitutes sensations" (Deleuze 1994, p. 78). While Kant supposes that sensations come to us spread out in a spatio-temporal structure as the *a priori* condition of all appearances in general, Deleuze's Humean conception of the imagination's passive synthesis conceives such a space and time existing prior to every experience as a biological function of the nervous system. As Deleuze writes in his Hume study: "the organism and its senses do not immediately and in themselves have the characteristics of human nature or of a subject; they must acquire these from somewhere else. The mechanism of the body cannot explain the spontaneity of the subject" (Deleuze 1989, p. 89). Rather, for the empiricist the organism's biological necessity transcends logical necessity. Space and time do exist with Deleuze, still, as *a priori* conditions, but these are never separated from sensibility itself. They are not the universal and necessary condition for every "possible experience," but space and time exist together *a priori* as a *"larval subject,"* as the spatio-temporal dynamisms of a passive self: "the passive selves were already integrations" (Deleuze 1994, p. 98).

2.3 The Larval Self: Contemplation and Self-Enjoyment

Having descended to the Kantian pathological, we cannot but grant that contemplation is inseparable from "enjoyment" and "self-enjoyment" (Deleuze & Guattari 1994, p. 212): contemplation does not merely contract material moments but it contracts the very matter of these moments (water, light, sulfates, chlorides etc.). In this sense each contraction expresses an enjoyment, not only on the level of our daily habits of life but on the deeper level of habits, on the level of primary organic syntheses, even on the level of the photosynthesis of plants enjoying their growth or flourishing. Compare the following passage from *Difference and Repetition*:

> No one has shown better than Samuel Butler that there is no continuity apart from that of habit, and that we have no other continuities apart from those of our thousands of component habits, which form within us so many superstitious and contemplative selves, so many claimants and satisfactions: "for even the corn in the fields grows upon a superstitious basis as to its own existence, and only turns the earth and moisture into wheat through the conceit of its own ability to do so, without which faith it were powerless…". Only an empiricist can happily risk such formulae. What we call wheat is a contraction of the earth and humidity, and this contraction is both a contemplation and the auto-satisfaction of that contemplation. By its existence alone, the lily of the field sings the glory of the heavens, the goddesses and gods—in other words, the elements that it contemplates in contracting (Deleuze 1994, p. 75);

with these two passages from *What is Philosophy?*:

> Plotinus defined all things as contemplations, not only people and animals but plants, the earth, and rocks. These are not Ideas that we contemplate through concepts but the elements of matter that we contemplate through sensation. The plant contemplates by contracting the elements from which it originates—light, carbon, and the salts—and it fills itself with colors and odors that in each case qualify its variety, its composition: it is sensation in itself. It is as if flowers smell themselves by smelling what composes them, first attempts of vision or of sense of smell, before being perceived or even smelled by an agent with a nervous system and a brain (Deleuze & Guattari 1994, p. 212);

> Even when one is a rat, it is through contemplation that one "contracts" a habit. It is still necessary to discover, beneath the noise of actions, those internal creative sensations or those silent contemplations that bear witness to a brain (Deleuze & Guattari 1994, p. 211).

Following Plotinus, Hume and Whitehead, Deleuze says that the contraction at the heart of contemplation is the highest degree of activity. It means for a vision to become what it envisions. Contraction is pure *becoming or individuation,* like muscles contract something of a wave of water to discover and learn how to swim. For Deleuze, it is Hume's genius to have shown how the contraction that preserves something is always in a state of *detachment* in relation to *action* and appears as a pure contemplation without knowledge: it is an unintelligible instinct. Deleuze argues this instinct does not require *having* a self as a center of action whose *being* is sensed as distinct from its surroundings.[22] Even if such an active self has already been constituted, it is for Deleuze always absent when sensation is felt as the pure deployment of the contracting imagination: the latter is situated on another plane than the plane, or order, of what is *constituted*, and is itself, in fact, without *being*.

Accordingly, the contemplative, larval self's empirical nature is not at all the empirical nature envisioned by Kant, that is to say the ego-centric world where impulses dominate. With Kant we find a simple—be it profound and fundamental—opposition between the animalistic mechanisms of sensible impulses *(Triebfeder)* and the freedom of rational will. But the *self-regard (Selbstsucht)* of which Kant speaks, and which he further differentiates as *self-love (Eigenliebe)* and *self-conceit (Eigendünkel)* (Kant 1996, p. 199), is *absent* at the sub-representative plane of contemplation con-

[22] The active self, on the contrary, will always rely on the implicit presence of the passive synthesis: "it seems that active syntheses would never be erected on the basis of passive syntheses unless these persisted simultaneously, unless they did not develop on their own account at the same time, finding new formulae at once both dissymmetrical and complementary with the activity" (Deleuze 1994, p. 99).

tracting excitations. The Kantian self-regard presupposes a unified self as a center of action chasing its impulses or other pathologically conditioned sensations. But at the level of contemplation contracting what Deleuze calls "enjoyment" there is not *first* a self that then chases, so to speak, its enjoyment. Rather, for Hume and Deleuze it is the other way around: the self is *constituted* on the basis of a contractile force which forms habits and as such these habits are the condition for a center of action (a Self) to emerge. While with Kant *pleasure* or pathological *gratification* is dependent on *re-actions* to excitations (e. g., I am hungry (excitation, displeasure), I search for food, I find and eat it which gives rise to pleasure), what Deleuze calls *enjoyment* is more like an emotion or an affective state. Enjoyment is not dependent on actions but solely on *passive* contemplation. This is why Deleuze, when exposing his conception of contemplation, always underlines that "it" (read: *ça*) takes place on a plane entirely different from that of actions and mechanisms:

> The search for sensation is fruitless if we go no farther than reactions and the excitations that they prolong, than actions and the perceptions that they reflect: this is because the soul (or rather, the force), as Leibniz said, does nothing, or does not act, but is only present; it preserves. Contraction is not an action but a pure passion, a contemplation that preserves the before in the after. Sensation, then, is on a plane that is different from mechanisms, dynamisms, and finalities: it is on a plane of composition where sensation is formed by contracting that which composes it, and by composing itself with other sensations that contract it in turn (Deleuze & Guattari 1994, pp. 211–212).

> It is a primary, 'true form' as Ruyer defined it: neither a Gestalt nor a perceived form but a *form in itself* that does not refer to any external point of view, any more than the retina or striated area of the cortex refers to another retina or cortical area; it is an absolute consistent form that surveys *itself* independently of any supplementary dimension, which does not appeal therefore to any transcendence (Deleuze & Guattari 1994, p. 210).

This conception of enjoyment means that its value is not yet bound to a self: it has not yet been *invested* in the psyche. In Kantian terms, it cannot yet be evaluated in terms of "interests" of reason or sensibility: the distributive rules constitutive of good and common sense (e. g., analogy) are not yet in play. The contemplating imagination does not know what its interests are. It is not yet an agent but a patient, like an embryo. Indeed, Deleuze conceives contemplation as a purely passive faculty of feeling that coexists with embryonic tissues. Insofar as it precedes a fixed sense of being a self, this most "primitive situation" of the mind and its enjoyment is *delirious*: it is pure change and indifference (Deleuze 1989, p. 23). From a *personal* point of view, the kind of sensation involved in contemplation is therefore strictly speaking *cruel* and *unbearable*:

> Embryology already displays the truth that there are systematic vital movements, torsions and drifts, that only the embryo can sustain: an adult would be torn apart by them. There are movements for which one can only be a patient, but the patient in turn is a larva (Deleuze 1994, p. 118).

> There are 'things' that only an embryo can do, movements that it alone can undertake or even withstand (for example, the anterior member of the tortoise undergoes a relative displacement of 180 degrees, while the neck involves the forward slippage of a variable number of proto-vertebrae). The destiny and achievement of the embryo is to live the unlivable, to sustain forced movements of a scope which would break any skeleton or tear ligaments (Deleuze 1994, p. 215).

If the human agent presents itself as a social, linguistic animal, the primitive "depth" of the mind must be said to be *delirious* in the sense that its unsettling breakthrough—for example in schizophrenia—is strictly speaking *inhuman*. The delirious energy in play in *contemplation* is not restricted to the human or even animal psyche (it is not only a psychic energy) but it contracts the very a-rational, errant, "demonic" distribution of energy that flows throughout all of nature (cf. 2.2).

On the basis of this intensive energy or "inorganic life" of nature, Deleuze distinguishes two primary developmental or individuating stages which biopsychic life goes through on the basis of *contemplation*: a first stage in which contraction is still an unregulated resolution of chaotic excitations and a second one in which it becomes *bound* to a reproductive *principle* of habit.[23] On the first, most rudimentary level,

[23] Note that we restrict our focus here only to the most rudimentary stage of psychic development based on contemplation, not taking into account the symbolic transformation of drives into desire and the constitution of linguistic, representational consciousness.

the contraction of excitation is not yet even an attempt at "mastering" the sensed energy. Such an attempt can only arise on the second level, when contraction learns and moves from a scattered to an integrated state of "binding" resolution, which *organizes* and gives a consistent *direction* to contemplation. Excitations become then "drives," which means that an excitation of the formed organism gives rise to a tension which immediately strives toward its resolution: it pushes the organism, which has become like a machine, to free itself from the sensed tension. Only with this contractile binding or "condensation" of a tendency does a larval mind emerge as a habit of living: "Every spatio-temporal dynamism is accompanied by the emergence of an elementary consciousness which itself traces directions, doubles movements and migrations, and is born on the threshold of the condensed singularities of the body or object whose consciousness it is. It is not enough to say that consciousness is consciousness of something: it is the double of this something, and everything is consciousness because it possesses a double, even if it is far off and very foreign" (Deleuze 1994, p. 220).

2.4 Sensation and the Aesthetic Idea

We have come to a point at which we can finally shed a light on Deleuze's conception of aesthetic ideas. The distinction between a free, unbounded form of contraction and one bound to an empirical principle of pleasure (habit) allows Deleuze to introduce a pathological form of contracting matter that is not at odds with the Kantian characteristic of the aesthetic idea of "freeing" the imagination from empirical interests.[24] The aesthetic idea induces a passage precisely from bound differences to a free state of difference. That which is *immediately* encountered in aesthetic con-

24 Cf. Deleuze 1984, p. 47.

templation (the *sentiendum*) is that which can *only* be "felt" or "sensed" *(senti)* and which gives rise exclusively to *sensations* in the strict sense, namely: *intensities* that *present unmediated differences*. As such, the encounter always suspends our psychic energy, introducing "unsettling difficulties into the sedentary structures of representation" (Deleuze 1994, p. 37).

One cannot understand Deleuze's conception of this blockage, the qualitative "leap" induced by the aesthetic idea, without addressing, finally, the relation between contraction and schizophrenia. In the schizophrenic experience, Deleuze and Guattari explain, the organism is lived like an enemy:

> It would seem […] that the flows of energy are still too closely connected, the partial objects still too organic […]. Desiring-machines make us an organism; but at the very heart of this production, within the very production of this production, the body suffers from being organized in this way, from not having some other sort of organization, or no organization at all (Deleuze & Guattari 2000, p. 8).

The breakthrough of schizophrenia always involves a certain struggle against the organism, which imposes an organization and integration of the organs. It is not the organs themselves which are the enemy but the "organization which imposes on the organs a regime of totalization, collaboration, synergy, integration, inhibition and disjunction" (Deleuze 2007, p. 20). For the schizophrenic, the energy of drives and desire are too bound, the objects of desire "too organic." Two tendencies result from this struggle: either the organless body of the schizophrenic renounces its organs, exerting a "repulsive action on them" which leads to a catatonic stasis of the body. This is the "paranoid form" of schizophrenia. On the other hand, the organless body can *attract* the organs, appropriating them for itself, and make them function in a regime other than the one imposed by the organism, as if they were "miraculously" born on the organless body. For example: "the mouth-anus-lung of the anorexic" (Deleuze 2007, p. 20).

It is precisely the "miraculous" non-organic functioning of the body which captivates Deleuze. Although the body-without-organs is clearly the unproductive and sterile *inside* all production, the stupor of all productivity, the organless body is nonetheless "pure intensive matter," a "stationary motor" labeled by Deleuze as "the death instinct" (Deleuze 2007, p. 21). Deleuze turns at this point to Freud's remarkable discovery of "secondary narcissism," which arises when the libido withdraws from objectal investments and retreats toward a "great amnesiac" self (Deleuze 1994, p. 111). Freud first discusses this discovery in an article from 1914 entitled "On Narcissism: An Introduction," which poses the following question: "What happens to the libido which has been withdrawn from external objects in schizophrenia?"[25] Aside from a state of "megalomania," the schizophrenic gives up his relation to reality, withdrawing his libido from people and things in the external world, without even replacing them by others in phantasy. This observation leads Freud to distinguish "a sexual libido from a non-sexual energy of the ego-instincts."[26] For Deleuze, the striking answer to the destiny of the drives is however only given in a later essay, "The Ego and the Id": "The transposition of *objectal* libido into *narcissistic* libido manifestly brings with it an *abandonment of the sexual goals*, a *desexualisation*, thus a kind of sublimation."[27] For Deleuze, Freud's great discovery is that of a *"displaceable energy"* which in retreating from an objectal investment becomes a kind of de-sexualized desire:

> The narcissistic ego has no more than a dead body, having lost the body at the same time as the objects. [...] It is this relation between the narcissistic ego and the death instinct that Freud indicated

25 Sigmund Freud, *La vie sexuelle* (Paris: P.U.F., 1969), p. 82. Cited in: Montebello 2008, p. 179.

26 Ibid., p. 84. Cited in: Montebello 2008, p. 180.

27 Sigmund Freud, "Le moi et le ça," in *Essais de psychanalyse* (Paris: Payot, 1982), p. 242. Cited in: Montebello 2008, p. 180.

> so profoundly in saying that there is no reflux of the libido on to the ego without it becoming *desexualized* and forming a neutral *displaceable* energy (Deleuze 1994, p. 111).

Yet, while Freud considers this reflux as a regression to a non-animated state of the organism *before* life, an attraction of the organism toward a primordial state of inanimate, inert matter—Freud took recourse to a mechanistic, Newtonian materialism—Deleuze objects that this displaceable energy unbound in schizophrenia is not an experience of "indifferent, inanimate matter to which the living would 'return'," but an experience of a "pure form—the empty form of time" (Deleuze 1994, p. 112). In other words, for Deleuze the death instinct expresses an attraction to the primary stage of contemplation, underlying the larval self: the *unbound* contraction of energy prior to the formation of drives or habits. For Deleuze, the living organism that is constituted upon contracted habits and drives always testifies to "the existence of another order, a heterogeneous order of another dimension—as though the individuating factors or the atoms taken individually with their power of mutual communication and fluent instability there *enjoyed a higher degree of expression*" (Deleuze 1994, p. 255, my emphasis). Attracted to this primordial level of morphogenetic energy, the schizophrenic body-without-organs is a kind of *traversal* of the self toward "*free differences* when they are no longer subject to the form imposed upon them by an I or an ego, when they assume a shape which excludes *my* own coherence no less than that of any identity whatsoever" (Deleuze 1994, p. 113). In his study of Bacon, Deleuze expresses his captivation for this "miraculous" non-organic functioning of the body as follows:

> The body without organs is opposed less to organs than to that organization of organs we call an organism. It is an intense and intensive body. It is traversed by a wave that traces levels or thresholds in the body according to the variations of its amplitude. Thus the body does not have organs, but thresholds or levels. Sensation is not qualitative and qualified but has only an intensive reality, which no longer determines itself representative elements, but allotropic variations. Sensation is vibration. [...] It is a

> whole nonorganic life, for the organism is not life, it is what imprisons life. The body is completely living, and yet nonorganic. Likewise sensation, when it acquires a body through the organism, takes on an excessive and spasmodic appearance, exceeding the bounds of organic activity. It is immediately conveyed in the flesh through the nervous wave or vital emotion (Deleuze 2003, pp. 44–45).

Thus, while the self certainly feels *exceeded*, the body-without-organs is still an intensifying principle, a positive power of inorganic life: it is desire in a *free* state, the stuff that makes up desire but not bound to a personal perspective, free circulation of energy. Let us not be misguided, however: insofar as it opens up a "secret coherence" beyond the self, the sensation of the animalistic, instinctive roots of the self is always felt as a violent shock (Deleuze 1994, pp. 89–90). It is the discovery that the morphogenetic powers of the larval self do not find their *finality* in the organism or in subjective life. Aesthetic contemplation is in no way a feeling of reciprocity between sensing and sensed, as in Kant's conception of contemplation. Such reciprocity does not isolate the productivity of nature *in* man, it isolates man in nature, it makes of nature a nature *for* man. But for Deleuze man has no kind of primacy. Art is always directed at the identity of man and nature. Accordingly, Deleuze inverts the Kantian *Gèist:*

> [Nonorganic life] attests to a high *spirituality*, since what leads it to seek the elementary forces beyond the organic is a spiritual will. But this spirituality is a spirituality of the body; the spirit is the body itself, the body without organs (Deleuze 2003, pp. 46–47).
> [It is] the power of a nonorganic life that can be found in a line that's drawn, a line of writing, a line of music. It's organisms that die, not life. Any work of art points a way through for life, finds a way through the cracks (Deleuze 1995, p. 143).

3. Conclusion

The difference between Kant's and Deleuze's conceptions of ideal animation is unbridgeable. For Deleuze, Hume's understanding of the imagination as an animalistic faculty of contemplation-contraction allows us to establish a distinction between a dynamic constitution of a self *(moi larvaire)* that precedes the constitution of the Self as a center of action *(Moi)*. Taking up—but not without transposing—Freud's distinction between the "Id" and the "self," Deleuze distinguishes a passive self that is formed each time when drives are bound out of excitations, from the Self as the unified center of action. Being pre-egological, this larval self is an impersonal contractile form of subjectivity that is concerned with only one single (passive) faculty: the creative binding of intensive excitations into drives, which Hume labeled habits and which form the first emergence of ideality. This faculty, Deleuze argues, does not presuppose any memory or understanding—contraction is not a form of subjective reflection in the Kantian sense—and accordingly this larval form of subjectivity can be ascribed to living entities that lack such faculties, such as animals, plants and even micro-organisms.

Crucial to this reading of Hume's theory of imagination is that the contraction of intensive excitations taking place on this contemplative level takes place *before* what Deleuze calls with Freud the formation of a "pleasure principle," that is to say, before pleasure has acquired the *value* of a principle. In Deleuze's terms, contraction takes place on a plane that is to be strictly distinguished from that of dynamisms, mechanisms, (symbolically formed) desires and finalities. A plane, in other words, where the contraction of excitation is not yet organized and *bound* to the interests and pleasures of a Self, but where contraction envisions only an augmentation of the *vital force* or *power* at the disposal of the larval self. In this sense, the faculty of contraction expresses for Deleuze a vital will to power that acts independently of an empirical pleasure principle: it expresses a kind of "enjoyment" deriving from bio-psychic individuation that is to be distinguished from pleasure. This distinction brings with it, however, that the power of contraction recedes for Deleuze to a dormant, virtual state once an active Self comes to occupy the plane of subjective finalities. Accordingly, accessing the energetic plane of passive contemplation where drives and habits are *created* rather than *chased*, always requires putting up a fight against the narcissistic Self, a fight which in Deleuze's eyes art extends us a privileged invitation to.

Along this line of thought, we propose to distinguish between Kantian and Deleuzian aesthetic ideas as follows: while the Kantian spirit as ideal animating principle of the mind derives from the figure of a contemplator who enjoys her transcendent *detachment* from the baseness of the nature of human drives, for Deleuze the contemplative self is directed to the idea not by elevating and detaching itself from the drives, but only on the basis of a forced return to a neutral, unbound state of libidinal energy. This entails a wholly different understanding of what it means to be animated by ideal sense: rather than being a process that is analogous to cognition, that is to say, *analogous* to the way we determine sense in the mode of determining an object, Hume and Deleuze argue that our animation of ideal sense is first and foremost rooted *in* the vital, bio-psychic drives of the subject, and not in the intellect transcending them. As Rudolf Bernet puts it in a passage that gave rise to the conceptual inspiration for this essay, "one must attempt to think this more elevated form of human subjectivity not through a transformation of the self, but through a transformation of the drive."[28] From Deleuze's point of view, aesthetic ideas do not purposively *confirm* our principal capacity to transcend the empirical self to the position of an autonomous, law-giving subject, they are not the outcome of an aesthetic,

[28] Bernet 2013, p. 18: "Il faut donc essayer de penser cette forme plus élevée de la subjectivité humaine non pas à travers une transformation du moi, mais à travers une transformation de la pulsion" (my translation).

purposive and playful use of the schematism, but rather they express vital forces that exceed the cognitive faculties by far. The Deleuzian enjoyment which aesthetic ideas induce in the contemplative soul can accordingly be defined not as an *intellectual, spiritual* pleasure (Kant), but as a desire without pleasure, an intensive emotion of libidinal energy in its natural, impersonal state.

References

Bernet, R. 2013, *Force-Pulsion-Désir. Une Autre Philosophie de la Psychanalyse,* Vrin, Paris.

Cassirer, E. 1957, *The Philosophy of Symbolic Forms: Volume III: The Phenomenology of Knowledge*, trans. R. Manheim, Yale University Press, New Haven, CT.

Deleuze, G. 1984, *Kant's Critical Philosophy: The Doctrine of the Faculties,* trans. H. Tomlinson and B Habberjam, The Athlone Press, London.

Deleuze, G. 1989, *Empiricism and Subjectivity: An Essay on Hume's Theory of Human Nature,* trans. C. V. Boundas, Columbia University Press, New York.

Deleuze, G. 1990, *The Logic of Sense,* trans. M. Lester and C. Stivale, The Athlone Press, London.

Deleuze, G. 1994, *Difference and Repetition,* trans. P. Patton, Columbia University Press, New York.

Deleuze, G. 1995, *Negotiations,* trans. M. Joughin, Columbia University Press, New York.

Deleuze, G. 2003, *Francis Bacon: The Logic of Sensation,* trans. D. W. Smith, Continuum, London and New York.

Deleuze, G. 2004, *Desert Islands and Other Texts 1953–1974,* Semiotext(e), New York.

Deleuze, G. 2007, *Two Regimes of Madness: Texts and Interviews 1975–1995,* Semiotext(e), New York.

Deleuze, G. 2011, *Différence et répétition,* P.U.F., Paris.

Deleuze, G. & Guattari, F. 1994, *What Is Philosophy?*, trans. H. Tomlinson and G. Burchell, Columbia University Press, New York.

Deleuze, G. & Guattari, F 2000, *Anti-Oedipus: Capitalism and Schizophrenia,* trans. R. Hurley, M. Seem and H. R. Lane, Continuum, London and New York.

Hume, D. 1909, *A Treatise of Human Nature: Being an Attempt to Introduce the Experimental Method of Reasoning into Moral Subjects,* Longmans, Green, and Co, London, New York, Bombay and Calcutta.

Kant, I. 1974, *Kritik der Urteilskraft,* Felix Meiner Verlag, Hamburg.

Kant, I. 1996, *Critique of Practical Reason,* trans. M. J. Gregor, Cambridge University Press, Cambridge.

Kant, I. 1998, *Critique of Pure Reason,* trans. P. Guyer and A. W. Wood, Cambridge University Press, Cambridge.

Kant, I. 2000, *Critique of the Power of Judgment,* trans. P. Guyer and E. Matthews, Cambridge University Press, Cambridge.

Lawrence, D. H. 1960, *Women in Love,* Penguin Books, London.

Lyotard, J. F. 1988, *L'inhumain. Causeries sur le temps,* Galilée, Paris.

Matherne, S. 2013, "The Inclusive Interpretation of Kant's Aesthetic Ideas," *The British Journal of Aesthetics,* vol. 53, no. 1, pp. 21–39.

Matherne, S. 2014, "The Kantian Roots of Merleau-Ponty's Account of Pathology," *British Journal for the History of Philosophy,* vol. 22, no. 1, pp. 124–149.

Montebello, P. 2008, *Deleuze. La passion de la pensée,* Vrin, Paris.

Parret, H. 1988, *Le Sublime du quotidien,* Editions Hadès-Benjamins, Paris, Amsterdam and Philadelphia.

Shores, C. 2013, "Self Shock: The Phenomenon of Personal Non-Identity in Inorganic Subjectivity" in *The Yearbook on History and Interpretation of Phenomenology 2013*, Frankfurt, Peter Lang, pp. 157–183.

Völker, J. 2009, "Kant and the Spirit as an Enlivening Principle," *Filozofski vestnik,* vol. XXX, no. 2, pp. 61–80.

List of Contributors

Wolfram Bergande

Wolfram Bergande is assistant professor of aesthetics at the faculty of Art & Design, Bauhaus University, Weimar, where he also serves as deputy director of the Bauhaus Research School. From 2005 until 2011 he was a lecturer in philosophy, cultural theory and aesthetics at the Humboldt University of Berlin and at the University of the Arts in Berlin. Research interests include aesthetics, the philosophy of art, anthropology, political philosophy and the philosophy of history. He has published *Die Logik des Unbewussten in der Kunst* (Turia + Kant, 2007) and *Lacans Psychoanalyse und die Dekonstruktion* (Passagen, 2002).

Stefan Kristensen

Stefan Kristensen is currently a senior research fellow at the University of Geneva. He holds a PhD in philosophy, awarded in 2007, from the same university and Paris 1, with a thesis on Maurice Merleau-Ponty and the problem of expression. He has widely published on the problem of bodily subjectivity, on the theory of perception and issues in contemporary aesthetics, in particular on the notion of the image. His publications include: *Parole et subjectivité* (Olms, 2010), *Jean-Luc Godard Philosophe* (L'Age d'Homme, 2014) and *La Machine sensible* (Hermann, forthcoming).

Claudio Rozzoni

Claudio Rozzoni obtained his PhD in aesthetics and the theory of art from the University of Palermo with a dissertation on Marcel Proust and philosophy. He then developed two post-doctoral research programs on the notion of the image at the University of Milan (the first starting from both Edmund Husserl's and Eugen Fink's works, while the second deals with Denis Diderot's Salons). He is currently a FCT post-doctorate fellow at the Nova Institute of Philosophy (IFILNOVA), New University of Lisbon, with a project focusing on the philosophical significance of the film image.

Louis Schreel

Louis Schreel studied philosophy at the Catholic University of Leuven and is currently preparing a joint PhD at the universities of Düsseldorf and Antwerp on the immanent sublime in Gilles Deleuze's metaphysics. His recent publishing includes: "Pure Designation: Deleuze's Reading of Hjelmslev in The Time-Image," Itinera. Rivista di filosofia e di teoria delle arti, Università degli studi di Milano, vol. 11 (2016) and "Empty Time: The Temporality of Self-Affection in Kant's Analytic of the Sublime" in: Daniel Blanga-Gubbay and Elisabeth Ruchaud (eds.), *You Were Not Expected To Do This: On The Dynamics Of Production* (düsseldorf university press, 2016).

Sjoerd van Tuinen

Sjoerd van Tuinen is assistant professor of philosophy at Erasmus University Rotterdam and holds a PhD from Ghent University. He is the editor of several books, including: *Deleuze Compendium* (Boom, 2009); *Deleuze and The Fold: A Critical Reader* (Palgrave Macmillan, 2010); *De nieuwe Franse filosofie* (Boom, 2011); *Speculative Art Histories* (Edinburgh University Press, forthcoming 2016); and *The Polemics of Ressentiment* (Bloomsbury, forthcoming 2017); and has authored *Sloterdijk. Binnenstebuiten denken* (Klement, 2004).